PROGRAMMING CURSES IN PYTHON

PROGRAMMING CURSES IN PYTHON

ALAN GAULD

Author: Alan Gauld

ISBN-13: 979-8-7088-8443-5

Table of Contents

Preface

I first used the curses library in the late 1980's, on old-style VT200 terminals on a DEC VAX computer running the VMS operating system and writing in C. These were forms-based business applications and within a few years were all being replaced by GUI-based equivalents using the shiny new technology of IBM PC compatible computers and the Windows operating system. The days of text-based applications appeared to be over.

Over the next couple of decades the GUI became all pervasive and the rise of the internet and World Wide Web seemed to further remove the need for curses and text-based applications. But the demand for terminal-based applications never quite disappeared and the familiarity with GUIs meant that users would no longer settle for primitive command line interfaces. They wanted tabular display layouts and to be able to use their mouse, which had become a ubiquitous part of the computing experience.

Curses therefore did not go away and remains the most common (and most portable) method of writing text-based applications for use in a terminal window where full control of the screen and cursor is required. This in turn has led several scripting languages to create wrapper libraries around the original C libraries and that includes Python. The documentation for that module, while complete and accurate, does not attempt to teach those new to curses how to use the module. There is also a Python HowTo document but it is both rudimentary and fairly terse, covering only a fraction of the module's potential. This book provides a more thorough tutorial on how to use the Python curses module to write modern terminal-based applications.

The book is loosely based on the Linux Documentation Project's "Curses Programming HowTo" document, written by Pradeep Pradala. Indeed, the original intention was to simply translate that document's code into Python from C. However, it quickly became clear that the Python curses module differed significantly from the C version and that a complete rewrite of the text would also be required. As a result this book follows the general structure of the original HowTo document and the code examples are largely based on the ones found there. However, several new examples and even some brand new sections specific to Python are included and all of the explanatory text is original.

I decided to publish the material on Amazon as a Kindle e-book and paperback simply because I felt that would a) give it the widest exposure and b) because it was simpler than any of the other alternatives I could find.

Structure of the Book

We start off by looking at terminal control-codes and how they change the terminal display. Sometimes you will not need the full functionality of curses, perhaps you only need to clear the screen or change the display text to bold. The raw terminfo functions found within the curses module suffice for these simple operations. However this is very limited in its capabilities and it very rapidly becomes difficult to do anything more complex.

We then turn our attention to curses proper. We look at the various setup options and something called the Python wrapper that removes much of the drudgery of writing a curses application.

The next section covers output and how to display text on the screen. That is followed by a chapter on reading input from the user and reading data from the screen itself.

Attributes are the things that control how text looks on screen. This chapter covers the basic text attributes and how to turn them on and off.

Dividing the screen into smaller areas known as windows (and quite different from GUI windows) greatly simplifies controlling cursor and text placement; this is the topic of the next section.

Attributes help make text stand out but colour takes things to a whole new level. This section looks at the slightly unorthodox way that colour is controlled in curses.

The screen is only part of the user-interaction story; the next 2 chapters look at managing the keyboard and mouse.

Controlling the display is useful but curses also lets you save and restore screen setups, as well as temporarily exit curses mode, perhaps to run an external tool. This is covered next.

Moving beyond the basic curses module we find the `panel` module which is useful for managing multiple overlapping windows. The `textpad` module provides a fully working text editor widget for curses and the `dialog` third-party library presents pop-up dialogs for common functions such as selecting files or error messages – all done from within curses. Two chapters are dedicated to these extended capabilities.

Finally, there are two full case studies. The first presents a spreadsheet-like table of values which can be selected, edited and totaled using the mouse or keyboard. It also demonstrates how curses can fit into a modern OOP style of program design, presented using UML. The second is an implementation of Conway's "Game of Life", which demonstrates some of the features commonly used in games programming.

Throughout the book code and other literal values such as file or module names are presented in a stylized font `like this`. Comments within the code examples are displayed in bold red.

The source code for the book is available as a zip file from the author's web site:

http://www.alan-g.me.uk/hills/PythonCursesCode.zip

Acknowledgements

Following an appeal on the Python mailing lists several reviewers sent comments on the early translations of the Linux HowTo document. Particular mention must go to Alex Kleider, David Rock, Cameron Simpson and Bob Stepp.

In addition to those, several questions were raised and answered via the mailing list and the contributions of Grant Edwards in particular have helped enormously in putting together the examples in the terminfo chapter.

You can send comments to the author at this address:

alan.gauld@yahoo.co.uk

1. What is curses?

Ancient History

Back in the mists of computing time – around the late 1970s – applications were run on centralized computers with users connecting via video display terminals (VDTs, aka VDU (where U=unit)). The user interface typically involved printing questions on screen and getting the user to type responses. Alternatively, textual menus might be presented and the user chose a number or letter to initiate an action. This was all happening sequentially using simple print and read statements. Meanwhile, the terminals used on mainframe computers permitted programmers much more control over layout, so that columnar layouts and cursor movement around the screen were possible. A similar level of screen control was obviously desirable on the mini-computers of the time, as used in the bulk of non-corporate enterprises.

It was possible to control the screen of VDTs using special control codes sent to the screen. One code might clear the screen; another would turn on bold or inverse display of characters, etc. The problem was the lack of standardization; every terminal manufacturer had its own set of control codes. The code that cleared the screen on one terminal may cause the whole display to flash red and yellow on another! If you didn't have strict control over the terminals used it was impossible to use these codes in multi-user applications. What was needed was some form of terminal database giving access to the terminal codes for every terminal type.

In the UNIX world that need was first met, in the late 1970s, by a system called termcap (terminal capabilities). The curses library soon followed and provided UNIX programmers the ability to create powerful applications that could display "windows" (really just boxes or areas on the screen) and read/write text within those windows. Text could be in bold, underlined or inverted and users could use their keyboard to navigate around the screen, not just along a single line of text. It revolutionised terminal-based computing with screen-based applications like text editors and word processors becoming the norm.

However, termcap had many problems, not least that it was unwieldy to maintain and easy to break. A new, more powerful mechanism called terminfo was introduced in the early 1980s. This, in turn, led to an update to curses known as ncurses which included even more powerful features such as the use of colours and eventually, the ability to interact with a mouse when the terminal supports it. (You can read the slightly more complex history of curses in your favourite online encyclopedia.)

From the early 1990s ncurses became the dominant mechanism for writing terminal-based applications and was ported to other operating systems including the VAX/VMS library that I used, as well as a version for MS-DOS called PDcurses.

Modern Times

Ncurses is still actively used in many popular terminal-based applications, including the popular programmer's editor *emacs,* as well as the mail reader *mutt* and the system resource monitor *top.*

Ncurses is written in C, but many programming languages have created wrapper libraries to enable the features to be accessed from their language of choice. Examples include Ada, C++, Ruby, JavaScript, Perl, as well as the subject of this book, Python. However, curses does not have it all its own way, more modern alternatives are available, such as 'blessed' (offering simple terminal control) and 'urwid', which is an event driven UI framework built on top of curses. ('Urwid' and 'blessed' are not part of the Python Standard Library but are available on the PyPi repository of Python modules.)

The Python language version of curses is included in the Python Standard Library for UNIX-like distributions as the `curses` module. While the module covers the majority of the ncurses library functions there are a few areas where it does not follow the C version, since Python provides superior facilities within the language. This document takes account of those changes and explains the Pythonic alternatives. There are also a few lesser-used C functions that do not appear in the Python module, although they can usually be worked around. One example, the missing `get_attr()` function, is covered in the text.

The official `curses` module documentation is primarily a reference and not very helpful to those with no experience in using curses. This is largely because the module is just a thin wrapper over the C library and the documentation merely indicates which of the library functions are available within Python along with their signatures. The user is assumed to already be familiar with the C version of curses and its usage. There is also a short HowTo guide on the Python web site but, while it will get a new programmer started, it does not cover many of the more advanced possibilities exposed by curses.

This book is an attempt to fill the gap. It starts with the basics and builds up to fairly complex applications with full mouse and keyboard control. It attempts to explain a little of what curses is doing behind the scenes, as well as highlighting common 'gotchas' that trip up new users. While this is a book for new curses programmers, it is assumed that the reader is already experienced in the Python language. No discussion is made of standard Python language features or idioms. If you are not familiar with Python there are many books available that will provide that background as well as a myriad of online resources.

Installing curses

Hopefully, if you are using a UNIX-like operating system curses will be installed by default and you will not need to do anything extra. You can check that it works by running the following code from the Python prompt:

```
>>> import curses
>>> curses.setupterm()
```

If there are no error messages then curses is present and you are good to go.

If you do get errors then you might need to install the ncurses C library and/or the Python curses module.

The ncurses C library is usually shipped with your installation. In the rare case where it is not, it will almost certainly be available through your package manager as `libncurseswN`, where N is the version number and on my system, at the time of writing, the latest version is 6.

If you are running an unusual or extremely minimalist operating system you may need to download the source and build the library yourself. But if you are in that position you are probably familiar with how to do that.

Note: For Windows users there are at least two ports of Python curses available but my personal preference is to use the Cygwin package, which includes curses in its Python bundle along with a suitable terminal emulator and bash shell.

2. Controlling Terminal Displays

As described in the previous chapter terminals (and terminal emulators on GUI systems) are controlled by sending control codes, or sequences of bytes, to the terminal. One of the most common things we want to do is clear the screen. On a DEC VT100 series (one of the most common terminal types) this is done by sending the control sequence

```
ESC [ 2 J
```

If you have a suitable terminal then you can try it out with:

```
$ echo "^[[2J"
```

The $ sign signifies the OS prompt, you don't type that!

The echo command simply sends the string to the terminal. The quotes are normal quote signs. Then, inside the quotes, the part that looks like ^[is the escape character, which you get by typing `Control-V` followed by the `Escape` key. Next, type a normal `[`, followed by a `2` and a `J`. Hit return and your screen should clear. All VT100 control sequences start with the ESC [sequence but vary in length.

The problem is, of course, that every terminal type has different control sequences. That's where terminfo comes in by holding a database of terminals and their control codes. You can then ask the database for the control codes for a given command (`'clear'` in the example above) and send the returned value to the screen.

Accessing terminfo from Python

The curses module provides access to the terminfo database via a set of functions starting with `'ti'`. The most useful one by far is `curses.tigetstr()` which returns the control sequence for a terminal feature specified as a string parameter. These functions can only be used after first initialising the terminfo database using `curses.setupterm()`.

There is a slight complication because of the way Python handles strings and bytes, so you need to convert the byte codes into ASCII strings using the `bytes.decode()` method. Here is a short example of doing it in Python at the interactive prompt:

```
>>> import curses
>>> curses.setupterm()
>>> print(curses.tigetstr('clear').decode('ascii'))
```

The first line imports the curses module. The second initializes the terminfo data structures using the `TERM` environment variable to get the terminal type. The third line uses `curses.tigetstr()` to fetch the codes for `'clear'` and converts them via `decode()` to an ASCII string for printing. (Note: you must use `'ascii'` (or `'utf8'`) for the decode step, other encodings may not work.) If you try it you should find it clears the screen.

If you put the print statement into a function called `cls()` you could call it any time you wanted to clear the screen. Similarly you could write small functions to turn on bold or underline text and restore it to normal. An alternative approach is adopted in the example below just to show alternative options. This will in itself spice up your command line applications significantly. The following example shows a very simple program using the terminfo functions to control text display.

Example 2.1 terminfo demonstration

```
import curses as cur

cur.setupterm('xterm')

bold = cur.tigetstr('bold').decode('ascii')
cls = cur.tigetstr('clear').decode('ascii')
normal = cur.tigetstr('sgr0').decode('ascii')

print(cls)
name = input("Hello, what's your name? ")

print("Nice to meet you ", bold, name, normal)

input("\nHit enter to exit")
```

Notice that in this example we passed the name of our terminal (`'xterm'`) into the `setupterm()` call. This limits the applicability of our script somewhat since, if the terminal is not an xterm, it may not work as expected. It's usually better to rely on the default use of `TERM` unless we know that `TERM` is set wrongly. We store the various terminfo codes as string variables (`bold`, `cls` and `normal`) – incidentally the full set of valid string codes can be found in the terminfo man page. The first `print()` clears the screen before using `input()` to get the user's name. Then, when displaying the result, we turn `bold` on before displaying the name and then restore the display to `normal` afterwards.

It is worth pointing out that the ncurses documentation recommends using a function called `tputs()` to write the control codes to the screen. Unfortunately the curses module does not include that function, but using print directly seems to work for all practical purposes.

Although it's possible to do much more via terminfo control sequences this is about as complex as I'd recommend. For anything else it's usually better to jump into curses itself. So that's what we'll do next.

3. Hello World !!!

We will start in time-honoured tradition with a "Hello World" program which demonstrates the basic structure of all Python curses programs.

Example 3.1. The Hello World !!! Program

```
import curses as cur

try:
   scr = cur.initscr()              # Start curses mode
   scr.addstr("Hello World!!!")  # Print on virtual screen
   scr.refresh()             # Print it on to the real screen
   scr.getch()               # Wait for user input
finally:
   cur.endwin()              # End curses mode
```

The above program prints "Hello World!!!" to the screen and exits after the user presses a key (any key!). This program shows how to initialize curses, perform input and output and end curses mode. Let's dissect it line by line.

Initialization

To use curses you must first import the curses module. To save space on the page (and some typing) I will usually use an alias of `cur`.

The program starts with a `try:` statement, which is not absolutely necessary but, as you will see later, can save some significant issues in the event of an error occurring.

The function `initscr()` initializes curses and includes a call to the `setupterm()` function that we used in the terminfo example earlier. After the call to `initscr()` curses now manages all screen operations. If you try to use a normal Python `print()` or `input()` function inside a curses program it will not work properly.

Curses works with the concept of areas of the screen called windows. When you call `initscr()` curses creates a single window encompassing the entire terminal display and this is often referred to as `stdscr` in the curses documentation.

`initscr()` returns a new `Window` object representing `stdscr`. You should note that in C curses there is an actual variable called `stdscr` that you can pass to functions that require a window argument. In Python things are slightly different and `initscr()` returns a window object which you must assign to a variable that you can name anything you like. In this document I use the name `scr`, but you can use any valid Python variable name that you choose. However, the concept of `stdscr` as a window encompassing the whole available terminal space is important in curses so you will occasionally see references to `stdscr` throughout the text.

There are several other initialization options that we will look at later, but for now let's just use the minimal `initscr()` setup.

Displaying text

The next line `scr.addstr()` prints the string "Hello World!!!" on to the screen. This function can take various forms as we will see later. In its basic form, as seen here, it inserts its argument into the associated window object at the current cursor position. Notice that `addstr()` is a method of the window object returned by `initscr()`. In Python all the curses functions are either module level functions or methods of the Window class.

Since we haven't yet moved the cursor anywhere our present co-ordinates are at (`0,0`), the string is therefore inserted at the top-left corner of the window.

This brings us to `scr.refresh()`. When we called `scr.addstr()` the data is actually written to a memory buffer in the window object. In order to show it on the screen, we need to call `scr.refresh()` and tell the curses system to display the contents of the buffer on the physical display. It's a good idea to call `refresh()` just before reading user input, to ensure the user can see any prompts on the screen. In practice, the most common input method `getch()` actually does a refresh automatically but, as things get more complex it's best to call `refresh()` explicitly. Develop the habit now and you'll have fewer problems in the future!

The idea is to allow the programmer to do multiple updates on the window object and then do a single refresh once all the updates are ready. `scr.refresh()` checks the window contents and only updates the areas that have changed. (You can force a full window refresh by calling the `scr.touchwin()` function before `scr.refresh().)` Forgetting to call `scr.refresh()` after doing some updates and then wondering why nothing changes on the screen is a common problem in curses programming.

Reading character input

The penultimate function is `scr.getch()` which, as the name suggests, reads a character. Note that it does not, by default, wait for the enter key; it reads each keypress as it is performed. It does, however, block until a keypress is present. In this case we ignore the character because we are only using it as a pause before ending the program.

Exiting curses

It is very important to exit curses cleanly at the end of your program. If you don't your terminal is very likely to behave strangely after the program quits. `cur.endwin()` deletes all the curses data structures and puts the terminal back in its normal mode. If your program does exit prematurely, so that `endwin()` is not called, you may need to type one or more of the following commands:

```
$ stty sane
$ stty echo -nl
$ stty reset
```

to reset your terminal so that it displays properly. If that fails then you will probably need to close the terminal and open a new one! This is why we wrapped the code in a `try:` block and use a `finally:` clause to ensure that `endwin()` is called even in the event of an error.

Python provides a more convenient mechanism for running curses programs that we will introduce at the end of our discussion of initialization, which is the subject of the next chapter.

4. Initialization

Our "Hello World" example in the previous chapter showed the most basic form of initialization required by all curses programs, namely calling `curses.initscr()`. There are however several other functions which can be called after this to control the behaviour of the terminal. Some of the features that can be selected include the use of Function Keys, the mouse, colours, special control sequences (such as Ctrl-C to interrupt the program) and whether the characters typed are displayed to the screen (echo). You can also control how the input functions react: whether they wait for a single character to be typed, or a full line, or whether they immediately read the current keyboard state before returning to the program.

Many of these functions are not only used at initialization but can be used during a program as well. For example, a password reading function might turn off screen echoing until the password has been read, and then turn it back on for normal use. However, it is normal practice to set up the terminal at the start of the program so we will treat them all as initializers for the moment.

We will now consider each of these functions in turn and conclude with a unique Python feature which simplifies the whole curses initialization and finalization process. But first we need to talk about terminal modes.

Terminal modes

In curses programming, the terminal can be in one of three modes. These are raw, cbreak (aka semi-cooked) and normal (aka cooked).

- **raw mode:** all input characters are passed directly to curses. This includes control sequences such as Ctrl-C or Ctrl-Z. The programmer is responsible for handling any possible keyboard input.
- **cbreak mode:** identical to raw mode except that control sequences are passed to the operating system, so Ctrl-C will interrupt your program and Ctrl-Z will suspend it, unlike raw mode. The flow control commands – Ctrl-S to pause and Ctrl-Q to continue – also work in cbreak mode.
- **normal mode:** buffers input characters until a carriage return (or EOF) is detected. It then passes the string to curses for processing. Ctrl characters are passed to the operating system as for cbreak mode. Basic editing of the input line is possible (backspace and insert/delete characters, etc.). This may sound like a good idea but, in practice, is difficult to manage since, if you try to read a single character, the user can type a string and curses will then return the first character of that string. But the other characters are still in the buffer, so next time you ask to read a character you will not fetch any input from the user, instead curses will simply return the second character from the initial string. This is rarely what you want.

Normal mode is a slightly confusing name since it sounds like what curses should normally be in, but it's not. Instead the normal refers to the terminal mode when not running curses! By turning normal mode on during a curses session you get a non-curses-like experience.

The default mode in Python after `initscr()` is called is cbreak mode.

`raw()` and `noraw()`

The default terminal behaviour (outside curses) reads input characters into a buffer and waits until it sees a carriage return (usually via the Enter key). However, some characters have special meaning, for example Ctrl-C usually interrupts a program and Ctrl-Z suspends it.

Often in a curses program we use an event-loop style of programming to read and process characters and want to take full control of the keyboard input ourselves. That's where raw mode comes in. Raw mode sends all characters directly to our program one character at a time. If you want to process Ctrl-C or Ctrl-Z you must detect and deal with those characters in your code. `noraw()` returns you to normal mode.

`cbreak()` and `nocbreak()`

This is like raw mode but the special control character sequences are passed to the operating system. So no line buffering takes place (like raw), but control sequences are passed to the OS (like no raw). Note that in Python Ctrl-C will raise a `KeyboardInterrupt` error so a `try/finally` can ensure that `endwin()` is still called before the program exits. Calling `nocbreak()` will put the terminal in "normal mode".

`echo()` and `noecho()`

This pair of functions turns echoing of input characters on or off. When echo is on, any characters typed at the keyboard will be displayed, or echoed, to the screen. With echo off, the cursor remains where it is and nothing is displayed.

This is often used in games where characters are read to control the action but we do not want to display them on screen. Another advantage of noecho is that you can control what is echoed and where; the cursor does not move but the output can be placed anywhere on the screen. It requires a lot more effort by the programmer of course but does offer more precise control.

Note that these functions operate at the terminal level, you cannot control echo for a single window within the screen, it is all or nothing.

The default setting is echo on.

keypad()

This method enables the reading of function keys like F1, F2, arrow keys, mouse clicks etc. You will want to turn this on for most programs because users expect to be able to use arrow keys to move around the screen and the function keys are often used for special operations (e.g. F1 traditionally displays a help screen). If you want to offer mouse support you must turn this on.

Call `window.keypad(True)` to enable this feature for any given window. You will learn more about key management in later sections of this document. Note that it is window specific so if you are using multiple windows and find that you are not able to recognize the special keys (or mouse clicks) check that you have set this for the window in question. If you do want to turn it off for some reason then call `window.keypad(False)`.

`halfdelay()`

Half-delay mode is a variation on cbreak mode in that characters typed are immediately available to the program, however halfdelay adds a time delay of 'X' tenths of a second and then returns `ERR`, if no input is available. 'X' is the timeout value passed to the function `halfdelay()`. Using halfdelay mode prevents the user interface becoming unresponsive if the user does not press a key in a timely manner (for example clocks or progress trackers can be updated).

To get out of halfdelay mode you must call `nocbreak()`. If you then want to continue in true cbreak mode you need to follow that immediately by a call to `cbreak()`, which can seem rather non-intuitive but is necessary. Mostly you won't need to use halfdelay mode. Notice that `halfdelay()` is a terminal level setting; it is not specific to a window.

`nodelay()`

Generally, when you call `window.getch()` curses will block until the user enters a keystroke (or mouse click) – see `halfdelay()` above. However, it is possible to turn the blocking off and, in that case, `getch()` will return any key that is pressed at the time it is called or return `-1` if no key is pressed. (Users of old BASIC interpreters will recognize this behaviour as the same as the `INKEY$` function of BASIC). This can occasionally be useful for games (or real-time control applications) where you want to see if the user is doing something without holding up the action.

You turn off blocking with a call to `window.nodelay(True)` and turn it back on again using `window.nodelay(False)`.

Note that `nodelay()` is a window method and only applies to the specific window for which it is called.

`scrollok()`

This is a window method that is used to turn on/off the ability of the window to scroll. If you add text beyond the bottom right position in a window it usually generates an error. However, if `scrollok(True)` has been called the window will scroll up to create a new line and the text will wrap around. The line at the top of the window will be lost.

Scrolling is turned off by calling `scrollok(False)`. The default is for scrolling to be off.

Miscellaneous Initialization Functions

There are a few more functions which are sometimes used during initialization to customize curses' behaviour. Examples include setting the tab size or turning on or off newline mode. These are rarely used in modern terminal code but are described in the `curses` module documentation.

Two specific areas of initialization will be left till later; these are colour handling and mouse control. They will be discussed separately, in their own chapters.

An Example

Let's write a program that will demonstrate the usage of these functions and the different terminal mode behaviours that result. It is recommended that you play with this example code, turning on and off the various modes and observing closely the changes in behaviour. In particular you will need to try typing multiple and single characters and using control sequences. Observe closely the output that is printed each time.

Example 4.1. Terminal modes example

```
import curses as cur

ch = -1
delay = True

try:
   scr = cur.initscr()
   #cur.nocbreak() # put in normal mode
   #cur.raw()      # put in raw mode
   #cur.cbreak()   # put in cbreak mode
   #scr.nodelay(True) ; delay = False  # turn on nodelay mode

   scr.addstr("Type something here: ")
   scr.refresh()
   if delay:
      ch = scr.getch()
   else:
      while ch == -1: ch = scr.getch()
   scr.addstr("\nYou typed: %s" % chr(ch))
   scr.refresh()
   cur.napms(1000) # sleep for 1s so we can see the output
finally:
   cur.endwin()
```

You will see several lines that are commented out. By un-commenting one of them you will change the terminal mode. With all of them commented out you will be in cbreak mode, the default after `initscr()`. You could add code to try halfdelay and noecho modes too if you wish.

One point to note is the use of `napms()` to create a delay before exiting the program. If you find the delay too short simply change the argument to a higher number of milliseconds. `napms()` can be a useful tool while debugging curses programs.

The curses.wrapper() function

A unique feature to the Python version of curses is the wrapper functionality. So far, every program we have written has included the standard `initscr()` and `endwin()` top and tail code as well as other initialization type things. To save us having to type this every time, Python provides a convenience function that takes care of all the standard initialization and then calls a function that takes a window as its only argument.

The wrapper also catches any errors and ensures that `endwin()` gets called to clean up the screen for us. In the examples from here on I'll usually use the wrapper for convenience unless there is some specific initialization that needs doing or we are omitting some of the usual initialization steps.

There is one default option which might catch you out, namely that the wrapper chooses to turn echo off. This is a slightly odd choice but you must remember to call `curses.echo()` if you want it turned on.

Here is a minimal example using the wrapper:

Example 4.2 – Python wrapper example

```
import curses as cur

def main(scr):
   scr.addstr("Hello world")
   scr.refresh()
   scr.getch()

cur.wrapper(main)
```

A Word about Windows

Windows are fundamental to curses. Almost all of the functions that read and write to the screen do so through a window. However, before we start considering these functions in detail, it is important to understand what that means. Curses' concept of a Window is quite different to the windows you are likely familiar with in a GUI. For a start curses windows are inside a character based display, they are not therefore pixel based, they are character based. Curses windows do not have, by default, any borders or control buttons to move, maximise or minimise them. They are simply areas within the terminal screen. We have already mentioned the `stdscr` window that is returned by `initscr()`. It represents the entire terminal area. We can also create smaller -windows within that. Common reasons for doing so are to create reserved areas of the screen for menus or status bars, etc.

You can even create sub-windows within other windows to arbitrary levels of complexity (although being limited to character representation the smallest window you can use is a single character in size). There are also subtle variations in types of window, for example you can create new windows or sub-windows inside an existing window and these affect how the window coordinates are specified and what happens when the underlying window is moved.

Another oddity with curses' windows is the coordinate system. Positions on the screen are accessed via a y,x pair of coordinates starting at `0,0` on the top left and extending to `curses.LINES,curses.COLS` in the bottom right. `LINES` and `COLS` are the sizes of `stdscr` and are initialized by the call to `initscr()`. Notice that it is y before x for the coordinates, which is the reverse of the normal x,y pairing we expect from traditional geometry.

The most important point about windows for Python users is that the functions that operate on windows are all defined as methods of a window class. Unfortunately the class is rather obscured so the normal techniques used for looking at its attributes etc. won't work. But if you are curious try the following short program:

Example 4.3 Window class attributes/methods listing.

```
import curses

def main(win):
    help(win.__class__)

curses.wrapper(main)
```

We will cover most of these methods and attributes in the course of the book and there is a whole chapter discussing windows in much more depth. However, a few functions will remain uncharted territory for exploration by the adventurous.

5. Output Functions

Output is probably the most important feature of any programming environment since, without output, there would be little point to most programs (real-time control aside perhaps!). In this chapter we will look at how to display characters on a curses window. We have already seen the `addstr()` function at work but, as you'll see, curses has several other options and even `addstr()` has a few extra tricks up its sleeve.

There are four categories of method by which you can display characters on a window.

- `Window.addch([y,x, ]ch[, attr])`
  Print a single character with optional attributes at an optional location.
- `Window.addstr([y,x, ]string[, attr])`
  Print a string with optional attributes at an optional location.
- `Window.insch([y,x, ]ch[, attr])`
  Insert a single character with optional attributes at an optional location.
- `Window.insstr([y,x, ]str[, attr])`
  Insert a string with optional attributes at an optional location.

The first thing to notice is that all of these methods take an optional pair of coordinates so that the characters can appear anywhere within the window. If you don't provide coordinates the current cursor position is used. At the end of the add operations the cursor is located at the end of the string. The insert operations do not move the cursor (other than to the insertion location specified), it remains at the start of the inserted characters.

Also note once more that the coordinates are passed as y,x rather than the more usual x,y. This is just a foible of the curses library, you will get used to it eventually!

The `addXXX` family put the characters directly to the screen overwriting any existing text. The `insXXX` methods insert the characters, pushing existing text to the right. Any characters pushed off the screen are lost (it does not wrap to the next line) and will not be restored if the inserted characters are later deleted. That means that if you are using the insertion methods you may need to store the end characters somewhere so you can put them back if needed.

Note also that in Python we can do string formatting on the string object just prior to, or even at the same time as, sending it to the `addstr()` or `insstr()` methods.

Let's look at each of these methods in more detail.

`addch()` Method

This method puts a single character into the specified (or current) cursor location and advances the position of the cursor. (Remember that in Python a character is simply a string of length 1, it is not a separate type as in C.) You provide the character to be printed. In practice `addch()` is most commonly used to print a character with some specific attributes such as bold or inverse. (Attributes are explained in detail in a later chapter.) You cannot pass an empty string as the character.

If a character is associated with an attribute (bold, reverse video etc.), then curses prints the character with that attribute.

In order to combine a character with some attributes, you have two options:

- Pass a bitwise OR of all the required attributes as a final argument to `scr.addch()` (or `addstr()`) These attribute values can be found as defined constants in the `curses` module. For example, if you want to print a character `ch` in bold and underlined, you would call `win.addch()` like this:
  `scr.addch(ch, curses.A_BOLD | curses.A_UNDERLINE)`
- Use a Window method like `attrset()`, `attron()`, `attroff()`.

These methods are explained later in the Attributes chapter but basically they turn on/off attributes without modifying the characters in the window.

In addition to text, curses provides some special characters for character-based graphics (these are known as the Alternative Character Set, or ACS). You can draw tables, horizontal or vertical lines, etc. You can find definitions for all the available characters and attributes in the curses module documentation. The ACS characters are not available in code until <u>after</u> `initscr()` has been called. The ACS characters are discussed in more detail later in the document.

Trying to add a character beyond the last position on the window generates an error unless the `scrollok()` feature is turned on, in which case the text is inserted and the window's contents scrolled up one line.

In theory we could do all the output we ever need using just `win.addch()`. However, if we want to print a string, it would be very frustrating to have to print it character by character. Fortunately, curses provides methods for outputting complete strings too.

`addstr()` Method

`addstr()` is used to put a character string into a given window and as such is by far the most frequently used output method. This method has the same effect as repeatedly calling `addch()` until you reach the end of the string. A closely related method in this family is `addnstr()`, which takes an extra integer argument, `n`, immediately after the string. This method puts a maximum of `n` characters into the window. (If `n` is negative, the entire string is added so it acts like the `addstr()` method). Both variants can also accept an attribute value, which is applied to the whole string in the same way as discussed for `addch()` above. Likewise a coordinate pair can be applied to locate the string anywhere within the window.

Note that adding a string to the last line of the window that is too long to fit will result in an error unless the `scrollok` feature is turned on, whereupon the behavior is as described above.

In the following example you will see several calls to `addstr()`, both with and without coordinates.

Example 5.1: A simple addstr() example

```
import curses as cur
msg = "Just a string"

scr = cur.initscr()
rows,cols = scr.getmaxyx() # get number of rows & columns

# print message at centre of screen
scr.addstr(rows//2, (cols-len(msg))//2, msg)


# print message at bottom of screen
scr.addstr(rows-2, 0,
   "This screen has %d rows and %d columns\n" % (rows,cols)
```

```
    )
scr.addstr("Try resizing your window(if possible) and " +
          "then run this program again"
         )

scr.refresh()
scr.getch()
cur.endwin()
```

The above program demonstrates how easy it is to use `addstr()`. You just provide the coordinates and the message to be printed on the screen, and then it does what you want. Notice that it takes account of any newline characters ('\n') embedded in the string and responds accordingly.

`insch()` Method

This method is very similar to `addch()` above but in this case it pushes any existing text one position right. Any characters at the end of the line will be pushed off the window and lost. We'll use `insch()` in an example a little later, when we discuss the missing `get_attr()` method in the chapter on Attributes.

`insstr()` Method

This is similar to `addstr()` above but again it pushes any existing text to the right. Any characters at the end of the line will be pushed off the window and lost. A newline character at the end of the string will effectively be ignored since `insstr()` does not move the cursor to the end of the string. Newlines embedded in the string will however be recognized and treated as such, with the effect that all the text following the insertion will be lost..

There are other members of the `insXXX` group of methods that can be used for inserting lines. In this case the lines below are moved down and those at the bottom of the window will be lost. Consult the curses documentation for more details.

`hline()` and `vline()`

These two methods create lines. They take an optional position followed by a character and a count. The following code will draw a horizontal line half way down the screen:

```
scr.hline(cur.LINES//2, 0, '_', cur.COLS)
```

A Word of Caution

All of these methods take y coordinate first and then x in their arguments. A common mistake by beginners is to pass x,y in that order. If you are doing too many manipulations of (y,x) coordinates, think of dividing the screen into windows and manipulate each window separately. Window manipulation is explained in detail in a later chapter.

Another gotcha with curses is that if you move the cursor outside the window it will raise a `curses.error` exception. This means that any attempt to add a string in the last character position will result in an error as the cursor has nowhere to go after writing the character! (Inserting a string is OK however, because the cursor does not move on an insert.) This warning also applies to creating new windows and sub-windows, if they are too big or start in the wrong position you will get an error.

6. Input functions

If displaying output is the most important feature for useful programming then getting user input must come a close second! Let's turn our attention to the methods that allow us to get input from the user or screen. These methods can also be divided into four categories:

- `Window.getch([y,x])`
  Get a character, optionally from a location
- `Window.getstr([y,x],[n])`
  Get a string of optional length, from an optional location
- `Windows.inch([y,x])`
  Read an existing character, from a location
- `Windows.instr(y,x[, n])`
  Read an existing string, of optional length n, from a location

Note that the return value from `getch()/inch()` is an integer and values above `255` represent special characters such as cursor movement keys or function keys etc. `getstr()/instr()` return a bytestring object and so may need to be decoded to a string in the usual Python manner.

Note: The `curses.ascii` module can sometimes be helpful in interpreting the integers as characters, but is not covered in detail this book since it is essentially just a list of constant definitions many of which relate to old style teletype terminals which are no longer in use!

getch()

This method reads a single keystroke from the input. The input can be either directly from the keyboard or from an input buffer, depending on the terminal mode. (See the Initialization chapter for a reminder about terminal modes.)

In raw or cbreak mode the input is monitored and the method returns an integer representing the keystroke (or mouse click) as soon as one becomes available. If no input is forthcoming the program will block until some appears!

In normal mode (accessed by calling `noraw()` or `nocbreak()`) the input is read into a buffer by the operating system until an enter/return key (or EOF/EOT combination) is seen. The buffer is then presented to curses as input and `getch()` returns the first value in the buffer. (Remember that normal mode, despite the name, is not the default mode inside curses it is the mode normally used outside curses, that is, in the OS shell!)

If the `halfdelay()` feature has been activated, `getch()` will only wait for the specified delay (given in tenths of a second as an argument to `halfdelay()`) for your input and if nothing is received in that time it will return with a value of `-1`.

If echo mode is on the input keystrokes are displayed on the window and the cursor moved along one character at a time. If noecho is specified then the input characters are still read but they are not shown in the window and the cursor does not move.

If nodelay mode is activated the `getch()` method tests whether a key is currently pressed and returns the key code if there is one, or `-1` if there isn't. In this case you need to implement a loop that reads until a valid value is returned. The advantage of this method of entry is that in a program with regular updates, such as a game or progress indicator say, calling `getch()` does not cause the screen to freeze.

The return value from `getch()` is an integer. For ASCII characters the value is the `ord()` of the character. For most non-ASCII characters constants are defined in the `curses` module. For example the function keys are defined as `KEY_F1, KEY_F2`, etc. and the arrow keys as `KEY_UP, KEY_DOWN`, etc. By comparing the return value with the defined key constant, or the `ord()` of the required character, event handling decisions can be made. You will see many examples of this in the examples that follow.

There is a closely related method called `getkey()` that reads a single keypress but returns a string instead of an integer. This is significant because some special keys can return multiple byte sequences. Having a string returned makes character comparisons easier for regular alphanumeric values but less convenient for those keys with symbolic constants defined. Mostly you will likely choose `getch()`.

Finally, there is a method for reading so-called wide characters. `win.get_wch()` is the wide equivalent to `win.getch()`. We don't discuss the use of wide characters in detail in this book but you will find them discussed in the curses module documentation should you find a need to use them.

There is one final trick up `getch()` sleeves. Up until now we have been explicitly calling `refresh()` before using `getch()` but in fact we didn't need to because `getch()` actually calls refresh for us! `refresh()` is still needed where `getch()` is not used and does no harm if you do include it but, if you are doing a `getch()`, you can leave out the `refresh()`.

getstr()

As the name suggests this method reads a string rather than a single key press. This is the curses analog to the regular Python `input()` function except that you cannot pass a prompt string as an argument.

The return value is actually a bytes object which can be converted to a Python string by decoding in the usual way. `win.getstr()` does allow for some very basic line editing of input prior to hitting return. `getstr()` works the same way regardless of terminal mode, it always reads the entire string and it always blocks until input is provided. The only exception is that if noecho is active the input characters are not displayed.

Like `getch()`, `getstr()` does a `refresh()` before reading the input string. This means that any time you are getting input you can omit the explicit calls to `refresh()` that we have been using up till now.

An Example

Example 6.1. A Simple getstr() example

```
import curses as cur

prompt = "Enter a string: "

try:
   scr = cur.initscr()
   rows,cols = scr.getmaxyx()

   scr.addstr(rows//2,(cols-len(prompt)) // 2, prompt)
   bs = scr.getstr()   # read the user input as a bytestring

   scr.addstr(cur.LINES-2, 0,
             "You entered: %s" % bs.decode('utf-8'))

   scr.getch()
finally:
   cur.endwin()
```

Notice that we are using the optional coordinate values to `addstr()` to position the prompt in the middle of the screen. The call to `getmaxyx()` returns the maximum values of `y` and `x` for the given window, in this case the entire screen. Notice that, as is usual in curses, the coordinates are returned with `y` before `x`.

The `getstr()` call does not really need cursor coordinates in this example since the cursor will have been automatically positioned at the end of the prompt string by `addstr()`.

Note too that `cur.LINES` was used for the second call to `addstr()`. `LINES` is a constant, defined in the curses module, that holds the number of lines (or rows) in the current terminal. It is effectively the maximum height of any window and specifically the size of `stdscr`. There is another constant related to it: `cur.COLS` that defines the current number of columns on the screen.

In the code above we could have used `cur.LINES` and `cur.COLS` instead of the call to `getmaxyx()` however, if dealing with windows other than `stdscr`, you need to use the function as shown above, since they will probably not be the same size as `stdscr`. I used the two techniques here purely to illustrate both of the available options.

Reading from the Screen

In addition to gathering input from the user, curses also provides a couple of functions for reading displayed characters from a window.

- `Window.inch(y,x)`
  Read character (as an integer) from location
- `Window.instr(y,x, [n])`
  Read string (or n chars) from location

Note that the returned value from `inch()` is an integer in which the bottom 8 bits represent the character and the upper bits the attributes. The return value from `instr()` is a bytestring just as it was for `getstr()`.

Note also that `instr()` can optionally take a length value, `n`, as an argument in which case it will return a maximum of `n` characters.

You shouldn't need to use these methods very often but occasionally it is useful. We will see an example in the next section when we discuss how to get the current set of text attributes.

7. Attributes

Attributes are the way that curses controls how text looks on screen. They control the text's colour, emphasis, whether it is underlined or inverted or flashing etc. Of course, how much is possible will depend on what the terminal can display. As an example there is an italics attribute but not every terminal can display in italics, so if you try it will just be ignored in those cases, curses cannot add capabilities to your terminal that it does not already possess! The range of attributes available are listed in the curses module documentation and do change from time to time as new values are added. The most commonly used values are:

`A_NORMAL, A_BOLD, A_REVERSE, A_UNDERLINE, and A_BLINK`

It is important to understand that the attribute information is stored as a bit mask in the high bits of a character. When you read a character from the screen, with `inch()` for example, you read both the character itself plus all of the attributes that apply to it. There are some bitmasks defined in the curses module for separating the character and attribute data.

The mechanism for storing the attributes as a set of bits means that you can set/unset attributes using bit-masking techniques. In particular it is common to set multiple attributes at a time by using a bitwise OR (`|`) to join the values together. We will see several examples of this going forward.

In this chapter we will look at how to apply, reset and read the attributes in a window. We will not discuss colour because that gets a chapter to itself.

The following example demonstrates the use of bold text and follows the pattern of the terminfo example used in Chapter 2

Example 7.1 Simple attribute setting example

```
import curses as cur

def main(scr):
   cur.echo()
   scr.clear()
   scr.addstr("Hello, what's your name? ")

   name = scr.getstr().decode('utf8')
   scr.addstr("Nice to meet you ")
   scr.addstr(name, cur.A_BOLD)  # make it bold

   scr.addstr("\n\nHit enter to exit")
   scr.getch()

cur.wrapper(main)
```

Notice that we used the `scr.clear()` call to clear the screen and then utilized the `A_BOLD` attribute constant to make the output line bold.

This example demonstrates how the terminfo code can be simpler for this kind of basic text handling since it achieves the same result without the need to go into curses mode. But as we will see things can get more complex very quickly and then curses' approach makes much more sense.

It is very easy to get carried away with attributes and have bold, flashing and underlined text dotted around the screen. In practice such abuse makes for a garish display that is hard to look at distracting for the user. Attributes should ideally be used sparingly, only where they perform some useful role in drawing attention to some critical piece of information.

It's time to dig a little deeper into the world of curses attributes.

Attribute Details

We saw in the output chapter that the `addch()` and `addstr()` methods could take an optional attribute argument. We used this in the example above to turn the text bold. But what if we want to add a lot of characters and would like them all to be bold? Do we need to add the bold attribute to every string? Thankfully, no we don't. We can turn the default attributes of the terminal on or off without adding any text. Then all text added will have the new attribute settings. We will now consider some of the ways we can control window attributes.

termattrs()

The curses module provides the `termattrs()` function that returns the attribute bitmask representing all of the attributes that are recognized by thc current terminal. You can interrogate this (using a bitwise AND (&) to see if the attributes that you want to use are supported. For example:

```
atts = cur.termattrs()
if atts & cur.A_REVERSE:
    scr.addstr("The terminal supports reverse text")
```

In practice you will rarely use this since curses tends to degrade gracefully if an attribute is not supported. Usually the characters will simply remain exactly as they were before you attempted the change.

`attron()` and `attroff()`

The primary means of changing attributes, other than via the text output methods, are this pair of window methods. `attron()` turns attributes on while `attroff()` turns them off. Who would have guessed?! You can pass a single attribute value as an argument or you can combine multiple attributes using a bitwise OR (`|`). `attron()` is cumulative so calling it once to set bold then again to set underline will result in both bold and underline being applied.

Note that you can use `attroff()` independently of `attron()`. That is to say, you can turn off attributes even if they have not been explicitly turned on by `attron()` elsewhere in your code. Note too that turning on `A_NORMAL` is a quick way of resetting most attributes to their default settings.

Note that these methods only affect any subsequent text displayed on the window; the existing text retains its current settings.

`attrset()`

The Window class also provides the `attrset()` method. This works like `attron()` except it replaces the current attributes with those specified. This means that if we called it once with bold then again with underline then the result would be that the text would only be underlined. The bold setting would have been overridden.

`bkgd()`, `bkgdset()` and `getbkgd()`

These methods control the background appearance of a window. The background consists of a character (often a space) and a set of attributes (potentially including a colour).

The first two methods set the background while the last returns the current settings. `bkgdset()` only affects subsequent characters inserted into the window whereas `bkgd()` affects the whole window including existing characters. We use the `bkgd()` method in a later example to create some empty but coloured windows.

chgat()

The `attrXXX` methods all affect subsequent characters displayed in the window. They do not change existing text. To alter the attributes of text already on display we must use the window's `chgat()` method.

The `chgat()` method has several optional parameters:

```
window.chgat([y,x,][num,] attr)
```

The first pair is the location of thc characters to be changed, if not specified the start of the current line is used. If they are given, the cursor will be moved to the specified coordinates (i.e. to the beginning of the altered characters, not the end, as might be expected!).

The `num` is the number of characters to be changed, if not given (or given as `-1`) it applies all the way to the end of the line.

Finally the `attr` is the attribute set to be applied. Like `attrset()`, `chgat()` replaces all existing attributes with the set specified. If you want to change back you will need to store the original set first (see `get_attr()` below).

The following example demonstrates the effects of `chgat()`, watch carefully which characters are updated at each stage.

Example 7.2 Use of chgat

```
import curses as cur
```

```
def main(scr):
    scr.clear()
    scr.addstr("Hello, This is a test string...")
    scr.addstr("\nAnd this is another " +
               "underlined",cur.A_UNDERLINE)
    scr.getch()

    scr.move(0,0)            # reposition cursor
    scr.chgat(5,cur.A_BOLD) # 1st 5 chars on line
    scr.getch()

    scr.addstr(" oops! ") # overwrite first chars on the line
    scr.getch()

    scr.chgat(0,5,-1,cur.A_REVERSE) # reverse to EOL from 0,5
    scr.getch()

cur.wrapper(main)
```

Note that the use of `chgat()` does not move the cursor. The following `addstr()` overwrote the emboldened characters.

attr_get()

In C curses the function `wattr_get(win,...)` gets the current attributes of a window. Unfortunately Python's curses module does not provide this function. However, the attributes of a given character can be read using `inch()`. So we can create our own version of `attr_get()` like this:

```
def attr_get(win):
   y,x = win.getmaxyx() # how many lines in the window?
   cy,cx = win.getyx()        # store cursor position
   last = win.inch(y-1, x-1) # store last char on window
   win.insch(y-1, x-1,' ')    # write a space at bottom right
   ch = win.inch(y-1 ,x-1)    # read the char with attributes
   win.insch(y-1, x-1,last)  # restore last character
   win.move(cy,cx)       # restore original cursor position
   return ch
```

The function works by firstly storing the current cursor position and the last character on screen since they will be lost during the operations that follow. We then write a character, using the current attribute set, at the last position on the window. We can then read that character back using `inch()` which also returns the associated attributes. All that remains is to restore the overwritten character and then relocate the cursor to its original position using the `window.move()` method (We will discuss `move()` again in the Windows chapter). Finally, we return the character that we read, with its attributes, to the caller.

You might wonder why we didn't just read the character in the last position and use it? The reason is that it may have had special attributes applied earlier. By writing a default character we can be sure that the attributes we read are the current settings for the window.

Notice that we store the current cursor position as well as the character at the last position in the window and then restore them again at the end. If we did not the user of the function would find themselves missing a character and with the cursor at the bottom of the screen. Not at all what they expected! We will use this function, along with several other attribute setting functions, in the next example program:

Example 7.3. `attr_get()` and `chgat()` Usage

```
import curses as cur

def attr_get(win):
    y,x = win.getmaxyx()
    cy,cx = win.getyx()          # store cursor position
    last = win.inch(y-1,x-1) # store last char on window
    win.insch(y-1,x-1,' ')   # write a space @ bottom right
    ch = win.inch(y-1,0)        # read it back (with attributes)
    win.insch(y-1,x-1,last)  # restore lost character
    win.move(cy,cx)              # restore cursor position
    return ch
```

```
def main(scr):
    # This sets the default attributes to underline
    scr.attrset(cur.A_UNDERLINE)
    scr.addstr(0,0,
        "A big string which I didn't want to fully type.")
    scr.refresh()
    cur.napms(1000)

    # Store existing attributes (ie. normal+underline)
    atts = attr_get(scr)
    _,len = scr.getyx() # get x pos as length of string

    # Now call chgat to change to bold
    scr.chgat(0,0,cur.A_BOLD)
    scr.refresh()
    cur.napms(1000)

    # restore the original attributes
    scr.chgat(0,0,len, atts)
    scr.refresh()
    cur.napms(1000)

cur.wrapper(main)
```

One interesting feature here is the use of the `scr.getyx()` method. This returns the current cursor position as a `(y,x)` tuple. The x coordinate of the cursor is in this case the end of the string so we use that as the length argument to `chgat()` when we later want to restore the string to its original state. `getyx()` is one of several window information gathering methods that we will discuss in more detail in the Windows chapter, coming up very soon.

A Practical Example

It's time we started putting our understanding of curses to some practical use. The next example pulls together all the concepts we have discussed so far, including input/output and use of attributes. This will be the most complex example so far and the first that could be considered a genuinely useful program. The program takes a Python script name as input and prints the file with comments in bold. If the file is too long to fit on a screen we pause until the user hits a key before starting a new page.

Example 7.4. Highlighting comments in a script.

```
import curses as cur
import sys

def main(fname):
   in_comment = False
   scr = cur.initscr()
   rows,cols = scr.getmaxyx()

   with open(fname) as fp:
     body = fp.read()    # read whole file

     for ch in body:     # read a char at a time
        y,x = scr.getyx()

        if (ch == '#') and not in_comment:
          in_comment = True
          scr.attron(cur.A_BOLD)   # make comments bold
        if ch == '\n' and in_comment:
          in_comment = False
          scr.attroff(cur.A_BOLD)  # end bold
        if y == rows - 1:           # reached last row
          scr.addstr("<-Press Any Key->")
          scr.getch()              # wait for user to read it
          scr.clear()
          scr.move(0, 0)           # back to top of screen
```

```
                scr.addch(ch)
                scr.refresh()
                continue
            scr.addch(ch)
            scr.refresh()

    scr.addstr(cur.LINES-1,0, "Hit any key to exit")
    scr.getch()    # pause for exit
    cur.endwin()

if __name__ == "__main__":
    if len(sys.argv) != 2:
        print("Usage: %s <a script file name>\n" % sys.argv[0])
        sys.exit(1)
    name = sys.argv[1]
    main(name)
```

Don't worry about all the initialization and file handling stuff we have already seen. We couldn’t use the wrapper function here because we had to pass the filename as a parameter and the wrapper only allows for a single window argument to the function. We could have got around that using a global variable but using the full curses initialization code isn’t really all that difficult!

Concentrate on the `for` loop. It reads each character in the file and searches for the pattern ‘#’. Once it spots the pattern, it switches the `A_BOLD` attribute on with `attron()` . When we reach the end of a line after a comment it is switched off by `attroff()`.

The above program is really a simple one which doesn't do much. However, by adding to these lines one could write a more useful program which reads a file, parses it and prints it in different colours, just like a syntax-aware editor. One could even extend it to read other programming languages other than Python.

8. Windows

Windows are a fundamental concept in curses. We have already discussed the standard window, `stdscr`, which we have been using up until now. Almost all of the input and output and text handling features that we have used so far have been methods of the Window class. However, while `stdscr` is the fundamental window at the root of all curses programs it is quite possible, and common practice, to have several other window objects within an application.

Recall that a window in curses is simply an area of the screen. There are 4 types of window in curses and we will look at 3 of them in some depth. They are:

- A standard window (`stdscr` is one example)
- A sub-window
- A derived window
- A pad – a kind of invisible virtual window

We will first of all consider standard windows before looking at sub-windows and derived windows together. Pads are fairly specialized and not used all that often so I will conclude the chapter with a brief discussion but we won't be using pads in this book.

There are several reasons for using windows in your applications. The first is to organize the screen layout so that you as a programmer, as well as your users, can locate related information and navigate more easily.

For example one common screen layout has a single-row window at the top of the screen containing a menu of commands. There is then a single large window taking up most of the rest of the screen. Finally, another single-row window occupies the bottom and acts as a status display. This mimics the layout of most GUI forms type applications and so is familiar to users. Another approach is to split the screen in two, either vertically or horizontally. One window contains a list of items and the other contains details of the currently selected item. Think of email clients or file navigation systems as examples of this style. Finally there are games with all sorts of layouts including grids of cells in which different activities take place. Windows allow for these kinds of complex layout while keeping you, the programmer, sane because you don't have to track the coordinates of every bit of data on the screen, you can just refer to the particular window.

It is important to emphasize again that curses windows are very different from OS GUI windows. They have no frame or title bar or any other adornments. They certainly don't respond to the mouse or any keyboard shortcuts unless you program them to do so. They are simply a defined area of screen that can have text inserted, be moved, resized and so on. Having said that, it is possible to draw a border around a window to give it a more window-like appearance, but don't be fooled, the border is just text inside the window and unless you take care you can overwrite it or delete it.

Window Fundamentals

Window creation and deletion

To create a new window object call the function `curses.newwin()`. This creates a window object in memory which you can manipulate. `newwin()` takes a number of parameters, it looks like this:

```
curses.newwin(height,width [,top,left])
```

The height and width are mandatory and specified in lines and characters. If you specify `0,0` curses will fit the window between the specified start position and the bottom right of the screen. It is possible to create a window bigger than the physical screen, in which case you may find that your output becomes invisible! Let the programmer beware.

The optional top and left coordinates specify the top left corner position. The default, if you don't specify anything is to start at the top-left corner of the screen.

Curses will do its best to create what you want, so if you specify a window that is only partially visible, that is what you will get. A shortcut for creating a new full screen window is to call `newwin(0,0)`.

A window can be destroyed with `del(win)` in the usual Python style. It will delete the window object and free the memory.

Displaying output

When you first create a window there will be nothing visible on screen. The window does not change the existing underlying screen area. You need to add text or a border to the window first and then call `refresh()`. Without `refresh()` the changes will not be visible. This is where things can start to get confusing, you must call `refresh()` on the specific window object you have updated. Even calling refresh on `stdscr` will not cause a new window to be updated. That part of the screen no longer belongs to `stdscr`.

Adding text to a window is as simple as using the regular output methods that we have been using all along but attaching them to our new window. For example:

```
win2 = curses.newwin(3,30,10,5) # window 3x30 @ 10,5
win2.addstr(1,1,"A Window without borders")
win2.refresh()
```

Notice that `addstr()` uses coordinates relative to the window not the entire screen.

Window Borders

You can very easily add a border to a window using the `Window.box()` method. This draws a simple line around the edges. But remember that the line is inside your window and part of it, so if you want to display text in the upper corner you need to specify coordinates `1,1` to `addstr()` not `0,0` because the box corner character is at `0,0` and the top edge is occupying row `0`.

You can extend `box()`'s capabilities by specifying a pair of characters. (Specifying `0,0` is another way of telling `box()` to use its default border characters,) These are the characters that box will use to create the borders. Unfortunately the corners will always be the standard shape, which limits the usefulness of this feature!

But we are not restricted to the `box()` method to create a border, curses provides the `border()` method with much more control over the appearance. With `border()` we can specify 8 different values, one for each side and one for each corner:

```
Window.border(top, bottom, left, right,
              top-left, top-right,
              bottom-left, bottom-right)
```

However, in many cases `box()` will do just fine and is much easier to use.

That's enough theory for now. Let's try it out with a simple example program that creates a few different types of window, some with border and/or text and some without.

Example 8.1 Creating windows and using borders.

```
import curses as cur
```

```
def main(scr):
    # Basic borderless window on top line of screen
    w1 = cur.newwin(1,80)
    w1.addstr("window1")
    w1.refresh()
    cur.napms(1000)

    # Window with box border and text inside
    w2 = cur.newwin(3,50,10,5)
    w2.box()
    w2.addstr(1,1,"Text in a bounded box")
    w2.refresh()
    cur.napms(2000)

    # Default arguments creates full screen window
    w3 = cur.newwin(0,0)
    w3.box()
    w3.refresh()
    cur.napms(2000)

    # New window with custom border
    w4 = cur.newwin(10,10,5,5)
    w4.border('L','R','T','B','{','}','[',']')
    w4.refresh()
    cur.napms(2000)

cur.wrapper(main)
```

Window Management

Windows are not simply static areas on the screen. They are objects and as such can be moved, resized and cleared. Of course none of this happens by default, we must write code to call the appropriate methods. But it's much easier than trying to redraw the windows by hand in their new state.

The window also provides methods that return information about the window, most usefully its current location and size and the cursor position.

clear(), clrtoeol(), clrtobot()

This trio of methods clears the screen in one way or another. We have already used `clear()` which clears the entire window.

`clrtoeol()` as the name should suggest clears from the cursor to the end of the line.

`clrtobot()` clears from the cursor all the way to the bottom right of the screen.

We will use `clear()` regularly and `clrtoeol()` in a few examples, but `clrtobot()` is rarely needed.

move(y, x)

We have encountered `move()` earlier. It simply moves the cursor to the specified position in the window. Note that the coordinates are relative to the window not the screen.

If the new cursor location does not exist a `curses.error` exception is raised.

mvwin(y, x)

This method moves the window to the new location specified in the arguments. For standard windows the coordinates are relative to the screen, for sub-windows they are relative to the parent window.

If the window won't fit on the screen at the new location a `curses.error` exception will be thrown.

The other thing that will likely catch you out at least once is that the previous display of the window will still be visible on screen. To remove this you need to refresh the underlying window (which may be `stdscr`).

`resize(lines, cols)`

This method resizes the window to the new size specified. If the new size is bigger than the old the space (including the border characters) is filled with blanks. If the new size is smaller than the old the contents will be truncated.

If you have a box border drawn it's usually a good idea to explicitly redraw it after doing a resize.

As with the `mvwin()` method, the previous display of the window will still be visible on screen. To remove this you again need to refresh the underlying window (which may be `stdscr`).

`refresh()`

We have been using `refresh()` in all of our examples so far, it is essential if you want to see changes to a window on the physical screen. It's worthwhile pointing out that `refresh()` only updates the parts of the screen that have changed. This offers a significant performance improvement over refreshing the entire screen (or window).

Note that the documentation shows 6 parameters for refresh, but these are only used when working with pads, which we won't be using in this book. To refresh a window just use the default form of `refresh()` with no arguments.

Finally, a little bit about the underlying code. A `refresh()` does two things: first it updates the virtual screen, which is curses' internal representation of the physical screen. Then it calls a `curses` function called `doupdate()` that synchronises the virtual screen with the physical screen. Most of the time you can ignore this but we will need to call `doupdate()` explicitly when we get to the chapter on the `curses.panel` module.

`getyx()`

The window method `getyx()` can be used to find out the present cursor coordinates within the window. That is, the `y,x` values returned are relative coordinates not screen coordinates. Conversely, the window method `move(y,x)` can be used to position the cursor anywhere within the window.

`getparyx()`

This method gets the beginning coordinates of the sub-window relative to its parent window. This is useful if you have a dynamic sub-window that moves its position based on cursor or keyboard input and you subsequently need to find out where it is located within the current window.

`getbegyx()` and `getmaxyx()`

These methods return the current window's beginning and maximum coordinates respectively. `getbegyx()` returns the origin of the window with respect to the screen. `getmaxyx()` returns the size of the window in terms of lines and columns. We saw `getmaxyx()` used in an earlier example when calculating the centre of `stdscr` and finding the bottom line. But these methods work on any window not just `stdscr`.

`scroll(num)`

This is a method that is sometimes useful. Its function is to scroll the lines in a window up by `num` lines. The lines at the top of the window are lost. Imagine you are writing a logging application and want to insert the latest information at the bottom of the screen. If each entry takes say, three lines then you can scroll the terminal up by 3 lines then write the new entry in the, now blank, bottom 3 lines.

To make it work you need to first call `scrollok(True)` to turn on the scrolling capability, then call `scroll()` with the number of lines you wish to scroll (the default is `1`). You can also scroll downwards by supplying a negative argument.

`touchwin()` and `untouchwin()`

We said that `refresh()` only refreshes the parts of a window that have changed. This is good for performance but occasionally curses can get confused about what has actually changed and fails to redraw a window correctly. In that case using `touchwin()` will force curses to refresh the entire window. Be aware that the actual update on screen will only happen after the next call to `refresh()` (or `doupdate()`)

Its counterpart, `untouchwin()` has the effect of forcing curses to treat the window as unchanged since the last `refresh()` call. I have never personally found a use for this feature, but I assume there is one, or the function would not be provided! I only mention it for completeness.

Window Management example

This example illustrates most of the methods described above. It also illustrates how much care needs to be given to call the various methods in the right order. If you get a call in the wrong sequence you will usually wind up with spurious artifacts appearing on screen.

Example 8.2. Window Management example

```
import curses as cur

def main(scr):

   # Window with box border and text inside
   win = cur.newwin(15,50,10,5)
   win.box()
   win.addstr(1,1,"Text in a bounded box")
   win.refresh()
   cur.napms(2000)

   # resize and add string
   win.resize(5,30)
```

```
    win.addstr(2,1,"Resized smaller")
    win.box()          # redraw border
    scr.refresh()      # remove the old window
    win.refresh()      # draw the new one
    cur.napms(2000)

    # move to new position
    win.mvwin(20,12)
    win.move(2,1)      # position cursor
    win.clrtoeol()     # remove old text
    win.addstr(2,1,"Moved box") # insert new
    win.box()          # replace border
    scr.touchwin()     # force removal of the old
    scr.refresh()
    win.refresh()      # draw the new
    cur.napms(2000)

    # scroll window up 1 line
    win.scrollok(True) # turn on scrolling
    win.scroll(1)      # scroll the contents.
    win.move(3,1)      # go to "bottom"
    win.clrtoeol()     # remove the old border line
    win.box()          # redraw borders
    win.refresh()
    cur.napms(2000)

    # scroll window down 1 line
    win.scroll(-1)
    win.move(1,1)      # remove old border
    win.clrtoeol()
    win.box()          # redraw borders
    win.refresh()
    cur.napms(2000)

cur.wrapper(main)
```

Note the use of `scr.touchwin()` in the move section. We do this because we want to reveal anything that had been on the underlying `stdscr` window before we drew the window. However, since we did not directly change the area originally occupied by the window (`mvwin()` does not clear the old window display), `refresh()` does not know to redraw it. To force a redraw of the underlying `stdscr` content (which may include important text!) we call `touchwin()` followed by `refresh()`.

Also notice that the scroll operation scrolls all the text in the window – and that includes any borders. Curses sees borders as just more text in the window. So, as well as scrolling, we need to take steps to delete the border characters that have been moved into the display area then redraw the border around the window.

Derived and Sub-Windows

In this section we look at two closely related types of window. Both derived windows and sub-windows perform the same function which is to act as a window within an outer window. They are so similar that I will, for now, refer to both as sub-windows. The key differences compared to a normal window, as created with `newwin()`, are:

- Sub-windows share their content with the containing window. If you write into either the containing window or the sub-window at a position occupied by a sub-window the text appears on screen. You can then read that text, using `instr()` say, from either window. It is shared by both.
  To put that another way; if you create a standard window that sits inside the area of another window it will hide the contents of the lower window until the new window is either moved or deleted. If you clear the new window it will clear the new window but not clear the data below it, although it will still be invisible. However, once the new window is moved or deleted the old window content will become visible once more.
  If however, you create a sub-window on top of a containing window's content, the original content will be visible within the sub-window. The data is shared and can be modified via either window's methods. This is quite a strange concept and takes a little bit of getting used to!
- Sub-windows move when the containing window moves. When a sub-window is moved within its containing window its contents are not! Also sub-windows cannot be moved outside of their containing window.

The combined effect of these features is that you should treat sub-windows as defined areas of the containing window and once created not move them around. Consider them as being like static panels on a GUI form rather than as floating dialog boxes.

The advantage of them is that you can use them as an organising feature within the containing window. Consider a customer management application with a screen for displaying customer details: one sub-window holds the customer's name, say, while another sub-window holds the address. Yet another has a list of customer transactions. You can then write the address data direct to the address sub-window rather than to a fixed location within the containing window. If you subsequently change the layout of the form the code doesn't need to change other than the location of the sub-windows when they are created. The data entry code still writes the address data to the address sub-window and the text appears in the correct place. Without the sub-window every write operation would need to be modified with the new coordinates.

Sub-Windows

To create a sub-window you call the `Window.subwin()` method. It is very like the `curses.newwin()` function in that it takes the same parameters in the same sequence. There is one significant difference: with `newwin()`, if you call it with just 2 arguments those are the sizes of the window but if you call `subwin()` with 2 arguments those will be the location of the window. I recommend always calling `subwin()` with all 4 arguments.

The other gotcha with sub-windows is that the location coordinates are absolute, that is, they are relative to `stdscr` rather than to the containing window. Let's look at what that means in practice. Say you have a window called `parent` on screen, located at 4,4 and `10` lines high by `40` characters wide and surrounded by a border. To create a new sub-window inside this, taking up the top half of `parent`, we would need to call `subwin()` like so:

```
child = parent.subwin(4, 38, 5, 5)
```

That is the parent's height less `2` halved, and the full width less `2` - to account for the borders. Then the location arguments are the location of the parent plus `1` in both directions, again to account for the borders. It can start to get complicated and a diagram on squared paper is often helpful!

Once you have created your sub-window object you have access to all of the normal window methods. You can read and insert strings and characters and modify attributes etc. The coordinates used for manipulating strings and moving the cursor are relative to the sub-window, just as with any other window.

Just remember the caveat given earlier about the fact that these strings are shared by the parent window!

Derived Windows

Closely related to sub-windows are derived windows. These are created using the `Window.derwin()` method which is identical to the `subwin()` method bar one difference. The difference relates to the coordinates used when creating the window: screen-based for sub-windows, parent-window based for derived windows. Looking again at the example we used above, the call to `derwin()` would look like:

```
child = parent.derwin(4,38,1,1)
```

The size arguments are the same but this time we use `1,1` for the location because it is relative to the parent window rather than the screen. This has the significant advantage that if we change the position of the parent window (but keep its size the same) we don't need to change any of our `derwin()` method calls, they will still work. Personally, I tend to prefer derived windows since they simplify the calculation of coordinates. But aside from that there is really nothing to choose between them.

The following example illustrates all of the various window types in action.

Sub-windows example

Example 8.3 Manipulating derived and sub-windows

```
import curses as cur

def show_status(win, txt):
    # display text in bottom line of screen
    ht,wd = win.getmaxyx()
    win.addstr(ht-1, 1, txt)
    win.clrtoeol()
    win.refresh()

def main(scr):
    # create the main window
    win = cur.newwin(16,50,4,4)
    win.box()
    win.addstr(4,7, "Main window")
    show_status(scr, “Created main window”)
    win.refresh()
    scr.getch()

    # add sub-window of main
    sw = win.subwin(4,18, 6,9)    # use screen coords
    sw.box()
    sw.addstr(1,2, "Sub-window") # use sub win coords
    sw.refresh()
    show_status(scr,
              "Sub-window creates a view onto main window")
    scr.getch()

    # add derived window of main
    dw = win.derwin(4,18, 6,9)  # use mainwin coords
    dw.box()
    dw.addstr(1,2,"Derived window")  # use derived win coords
    dw.refresh()
```

```
show_status(scr,
   "Derived window is the same but uses relative coords")
scr.getch()

# add new window on top of main
nw = cur.newwin(4,18,15,6)
nw.box()
nw.addstr(1,2, "New window")
nw.refresh()
show_status(scr, "New window on top of main window")
scr.getch()

# move main window, including sub-windows
scr.touchwin()  # remove old window from screen
scr.refresh()
win.mvwin(2,10)
win.refresh()   # draw at new position, including subwins
nw.touchwin()
nw.refresh()    # but new window stays where it was
show_status(scr,
           "Move main window with sub-windows” +
           “ newwin is not affected")
scr.getch()

# clear main window - includes sub-window and border
win.clear()
win.refresh()
nw.touchwin()
nw.refresh()     # new window stays as it was
show_status(scr,
           "Clear main window text and borders” +
           “, newwin untouched")
scr.getch()

# redraw just the borders
win.box()
sw.box()
dw.box()
win.refresh()
nw.touchwin()
```

```
    nw.refresh()    # bring new window to top
    show_status(scr,
       "Redrawing borders shows window objects still exist")
    scr.getch()

cur.wrapper(main)
```

A Word about Pads

The only type of window that we have not discussed is a Pad. A Pad is like a virtual window that is not restricted by the physical size of the screen. Instead the screen windows such as `stdscr` can be thought of as a viewport onto the larger pad. Think of a GUI spreadsheet application like Microsoft Excel. The spreadsheet can have many more rows and columns than are visible in the Excel window. The user can scroll around to view the data. The total spreadsheet is like a pad and the visible part is the screen window. To display part of a pad you use its `refresh()` method with some pad specific parameters.

This is obviously quite a powerful concept and can be put to good use in handling large data sets or even in games. However, it is fairly complex to manage in practice and beyond the scope of this book. If you feel adventurous there are a few references to curses pads online, but they are relatively scarce and far from comprehensive.

9. Colours

Many early terminals only had two colours: green and black, white and black or yellow and black. You could decide which was foreground and which background but that was the limit. However, colour terminals eventually came along with a range of 8 (and later 16) colours so ncurses includes the ability to control colour. Don't get too excited though, this is not going to allow you to display bitmapped images or photos. Basically, we are stuck with those 8 original colours (and possibly additional limitations that the terminal type imposes).

The way that curses deals with colours can seem a bit convoluted. The concept is that the terminal supports characters and each character has a background and foreground pair of colours. These are known as a colour-pair.

A colour pair is treated as an attribute of the character, just like all the other attributes that we have already discussed. The number of colour pairs varies by terminal so there are mechanisms to query the terminal's colour capabilities but, in practice, you rarely need more than 8 (plus their reverse versions for a total of 16) and most terminals that support colour will allow at least 8 pairs.

The first pair (pair `0`) is defined to be white on a black background and you cannot change it. The other pairs are initially undefined and your first task as a programmer is to create the colour pair combinations you will need. There are 8 individual colours defined as constants in the curses module with names like `COLOR_BLUE`, `COLOR_RED` etc. You can use any two to create a pair so, if the terminal supports a total of 8 pairs, that gives you the potential to create 7 additional pair combinations using the 8 defined colours – that's a total of 27 possible pairs that you can pick from.

Note that it is, of course, the US spelling of `COLOR` that is used throughout the module code.

Utilising Colours

The first thing we need to do to use colours is to check if the terminal supports it! If it does then we have to initialise the colour system (basically a set of data structures in memory) and then create the colour pairs that we will need.

Once created, the pairs can be used like any other attribute. Let's look at a simple program that checks for colour capability and if OK then creates 2 colour pairs and prints a total of 3 messages each in a different colour:

Example 9.1. A Simple Colour example

```
import curses as cur

def main(scr):
    if not cur.has_colors():
       scr.addstr("Your terminal does not support color!",
                  cur.A_BOLD)
       scr.refresh()
       napms(3000)
       return
    else:
       scr.addstr("Your terminal supports %d color pairs" %
                   (cur.COLOR_PAIRS-1))

    cur.start_color() # initialize colour data structures
    cur.init_pair(1,cur.COLOR_RED,cur.COLOR_BLACK)
    cur.init_pair(2,cur.COLOR_YELLOW,cur.COLOR_BLUE)

    # Now display the coloured messages
    scr.addstr(2,0,
             "This string is in red!",cur.color_pair(1))
    scr.addstr(4,0,"This is in yellow/blue and bold",
             cur.A_BOLD|cur.color_pair(2))
```

```
    scr.refresh()
    cur.napms(3000)

cur.wrapper(main)
```

Notice that we start checking the colour capability by calling `curses.has_colors()`. This is a simple Boolean test and if it passes we can proceed to initialize the colour system with `curses.start_color()`. Now we can define as many colour pairs as we require, in our case just 2 new pairs.

`curses.init_pair(pair_number, foreground, background)` is used to create the pairs and assign them a number.

Once the pairs are initialised we can proceed to display output as usual. We assign colours to the text using the `curses.colour_pair(n)` function which returns an attribute value. We can combine this with normal text attributes, `A_BOLD` in our example, or use them in isolation.

Note that the Python `wrapper()` function calls `start_color()` for you so, if you are using the wrapper, you don't actually need to do most of the initialisation activity, you can just proceed to create the colour pairs you need. In practice you are unlikely nowadays to come across a terminal that does not support colour and at least 8 colour pairs, most have many more.

Changing Colour Definitions

We said that we were limited to the colours defined by the module (and what the terminal supports). That's only true to an extent. While we cannot add new colour constants, we can actually change what the associated colours look like! So, if we don't like the default blue we can change it into any colour we like! At least we can if the terminal allows us to. We can check that by calling the `curses.can_change_color()` function first.

`curses.init_color(color, R,G,B)` can then be used to change the RGB values associated with `color`.

Let's look at an example. Say you wanted to lighten the `COLOR_BLUE`. Then you can use this function as

```
if curses.can_change_color():
   curses.init_color(COLOR_BLUE, 700, 700, 1000)
```

Note that the RGB (Red,Green,Blue) values are specified from `1-1000` not the more common `0-255` used in HTML/CSS etc.

Note too that if you call this mid-way through a session any existing text in the specified colour is automatically changed to the new colour and the screen refreshed to display it.

You can see a simple example below:

Example 9.2 Changing colour example

```
import curses as cur

def main(scr):
    cur.init_pair(1,cur.COLOR_YELLOW,cur.COLOR_BLUE)
    scr.bkgd(' ', cur.color_pair(1))
    scr.getch()

    cur.init_color(cur.COLOR_BLUE,400,700,1000)
    cur.init_pair(2,cur.COLOR_RED, cur.COLOR_BLUE)
    scr.bkgd(' ', cur.color_pair(2))

cur.wrapper(main)
```

The first screen uses the original blue colour, then the second screen uses the modified blue colour.

Colour Content

Curses provides a couple of functions to query the current colour settings for both colours and colour pairs.

`curses.color_content(color)` returns the RGB values for a given colour number (e.g. `COLOR_RED`)

`curses.pair_content(pair)` returns the foreground, background pair of colour numbers (e.g. `COLOR_GREEN,COLOR_BLACK`) for a given colour pair.

10. Interacting with the Keyboard

So far we have covered all the main ingredients of a curses program. We have seen how to initialize the program, display characters using different attributes and colours, how to create and manage windows and how to read input from both the user and the screen. However, to really write a curses application we need to go further and consider how to structure our applications.

As you have seen we can use the `getstr()` method almost like the regular Python `input()` function. And the `addstr()` method can replace the regular `print()` function. By using these we can translate a regular program into a curses based application very easily and quickly. If all you need is to decorate your text output with some attributes, or perhaps control the cursor location on a single screen then that's all you need to do. But if your needs are more complex; if you want to utilize several windows and emulate GUI style techniques and style, what do you do?

If you have ever written a GUI-based program you will know that they are all based on an event-driven architecture and that is what we usually need in curses too. Unfortunately curses, unlike most GUI frameworks, does not provide that architecture as standard, we need to write it ourselves. That is the background to this and the following chapter. In this one we look at incorporating keyboard input within a large application and in the next we look at how to extend that to include responding to mouse clicks.

The Basic Requirements

Let's start by summarizing what we know about keyboard input. The simplest way of getting key presses is to use the window object's `getch()` method. `cbreak()` or `raw()` modes should be enabled when you are interested in reading individual key hits rather than complete lines of text. (`getstr()` will read complete strings when necessary and it has its own buffering mode) `keypad()` must be enabled to get the Function keys, Arrow keys etc. See the Initialization chapter for details.

When you call `getch()`, `it` will wait for the user to press a key unless you specified a timeout using `curses.halfdelay()` or specifically turned on the `nodelay()` feature. When the user presses a key, the corresponding integer is returned. For a printable alphanumeric character, the integer value will be the ordinal of the character. Otherwise the returned code can be compared with the constants defined in the curses module. For example, if the user presses F1, the code will be equal to the constant `KEY_F1` defined in `curses`. This makes reading keys portable and easy to manage. These constants include values for common control-key combinations as well as some shifted keystrokes.

If you want to compare to a text character then you will need to use the integer equivalent using the regular Python function `ord()`. You can also use the `curses.ascii` module definitions for some non-printable character's keystrokes not defined in curses, but these tend to be rarely used ASCII characters such as those related to terminal serial lines etc. The most useful is probably the ESC key code.

The following code snippet demonstrates the principle:

```
ch = scr.getch()
if ch == cur.KEY_LEFT:
    scr.addstr("Left arrow is pressed\n")
```

Let's write a program which creates a window containing a menu which can be navigated using the up and down arrow keys.

Example 10.1. Key Driven Menu example

In this example we create an event loop in which we continually call `getch()` and then process the key events. This is done by an `if/elif` chain, each test calling an event handling function or block of code.

```
import curses as cur

WIDTH=30
HEIGHT=10
KEY_RETURN = 10

choices = [
   "Choice 1",
   "Choice 2",
   "Choice 3",
   "Choice 4",
   "Exit",
]
n_choices = len(choices)
highlight = 0

def print_menu(m_win, hlight):
    x = 2
    y = 2
    m_win.box()
    for n,choice in enumerate(choices,1):
       if hlight == n: # Highlight the present choice
          m_win.addstr(y, x, choice, cur.A_REVERSE)
       else:
          m_win.addstr(y, x, choice)
       y += 1
    m_win.refresh()
```

```
def main(scr):
   global highlight
   scr.clear()
   # initialize application data
   startx = (80 - WIDTH) // 2
   starty = (24 - HEIGHT) // 2
   highlight = 1
   choice = 0
   choice_fmt = "You chose choice %d with choice string %s\n"

   # initialize menu window
   menu_win = cur.newwin(HEIGHT, WIDTH, starty, startx)
   menu_win.keypad(True)
   scr.addstr(0, 0, "Use arrow keys to go up and down. ”)
   scr.addstr(“Press Enter to select a choice")
   scr.refresh()

   # event loop
   while True:
      print_menu(menu_win, highlight)
      c = menu_win.getch()
      if c == cur.KEY_UP:
         if highlight == 1:
            highlight = n_choices # move highlight to bottom
         else: highlight -= 1
      elif c == cur.KEY_DOWN:
         if highlight == n_choices:
            highlight = 1         # move highlight to top
         else: highlight += 1
      elif c in (KEY_RETURN, cur.KEY_ENTER):
         choice = highlight
         scr.addstr(cur.LINES-2, 0,
             choice_fmt % (choice, choices[choice - 1]))
      else:
         scr.addstr(cur.LINES-1, 0,
                    "Character pressed: %3d" % c)
         scr.clrtoeol()

      # User chose to come out of the menu
      if choice == n_choices:
```

```
            scr.addstr(cur.LINES-1, 0, "Sorry to see you go")
            scr.clrtoeol()
            break
        scr.refresh()

    scr.getch() # pause a moment

cur.wrapper(main)
```

The first few lines simply create the menu and the `print_menu()` function draws the menu inside its window and highlights the current selection.

In the `main()` function we initialize a few more variables and create the window to contain the menu. We then turn on the `keypad()` feature for the menu window since we want to use the arrow keys. Recall that this is a per window feature not a screen level one so we must explicitly turn it on for every window where it is needed.

The event loop is simply an infinite `while` loop which displays the menu, reads a character "event" and then processes it.

Notice the `KEY_UP` and `KEY_DOWN` actions include menu wrapping code that ensures the highlighting wraps around at the ends of the menu movement.

Notice also that we test for key value `10` (defined locally as `KEY_RETURN`) as well as the symbolic value `KEY_ENTER`. This is because in most modern terminals `KEY_ENTER` is mapped to the enter key on the numeric keypad. Key code `10` (the `'\n'` new line) is for the more commonly used "Carriage Return" key. We could have imported `curses.ascii` and used the `ascii.LF` defined constant instead, but there seemed little advantage to that.

The last point to note is that after printing to the status line we call `clrtoeol()` to remove any characters lingering from previous messages on that line. This is good practice when messages of potentially varying length are being printed to the same line.

11. Interfacing with the Mouse

Sometimes using the keyboard is all that's required however nowadays users expect to use their mouse for everything, even in terminal-based applications. That's not a problem because curses supports detecting mouse clicks. It does not see mouse movement, so you can't draw lines or similar GUI style actions, but you can use the mouse to click "buttons" or menu items.

The Basics

Before you can do anything with the mouse you must enable the keypad feature using `window.keypad(True)` (also used to detect function and arrow keys) and the events that you want to receive have to be enabled with

```
curses.mousemask(mask) -> (available, oldmask)
```

The parameter is a bit-mask of the mouse events you would like to detect. By default, all the events are turned off. The bit mask `ALL_MOUSE_EVENTS` can be used to get all the events and is the most common use-case. The return value is a tuple of the currently available mouse mask and the previous mask. (This allows you to restore previous behaviour in the case where you only want a temporary change.)

The following are all the mouse events defined in `curses` (notice that there are no mouse movement events, only button operations):

Name	Description
`BUTTON1_PRESSED`	mouse button 1 down
`BUTTON1_RELEASED`	mouse button 1 up
`BUTTON1_CLICKED`	mouse button 1 clicked

BUTTON1_DOUBLE_CLICKED	mouse button 1 double clicked
BUTTON1_TRIPLE_CLICKED	mouse button 1 triple clicked
BUTTON2_PRESSED	mouse button 2 down
BUTTON2_RELEASED	mouse button 2 up
BUTTON2_CLICKED	mouse button 2 clicked
BUTTON2_DOUBLE_CLICKED	mouse button 2 double clicked
BUTTON2_TRIPLE_CLICKED	mouse button 2 triple clicked
BUTTON3_PRESSED	mouse button 3 down
BUTTON3_CLICKED	mouse button 3 clicked
BUTTON3_DOUBLE_CLICKED	mouse button 3 double clicked
BUTTON3_TRIPLE_CLICKED	mouse button 3 triple clicked
BUTTON4_PRESSED	mouse button 4 down
BUTTON4_RELEASED	mouse button 4 up
BUTTON4_CLICKED	mouse button 4 clicked
BUTTON4_DOUBLE_CLICKED	mouse button 4 double clicked
BUTTON4_TRIPLE_CLICKED	mouse button 4 triple clicked
BUTTON_SHIFT	shift was down during button state change
BUTTON_CTRL	control was down during button state change
BUTTON_ALT	alt was down during button state change
ALL_MOUSE_EVENTS	report all button state changes
REPORT_MOUSE_POSITION	report mouse movement

Getting Events

Once the `mousemask()` function has read the event mask the `getch()` method will return `KEY_MOUSE` every time one of the registered mouse events occurs. Then the mouse event can be retrieved with `curses.getmouse()`.

`curses.getmouse()` returns the event as a 5-tuple: `(Id,X,Y,Z,bstate)`

The `bstate` is the main value we are interested in. It tells us the button state of the mouse, that is, which button was pressed. The `Id` is for handling multiple input devices and the `Z` coordinate is not currently used. `X,Y` give the screen coordinates where the event occurred. (Note that the mouse event returns `X` before `Y` unlike most curses functions.) We use the `bstate` information by performing a bitwise AND (`&`) with the mouse event definitions above.

The general code structure looks like this:

```
ch = win.getch()
if ch == cur.KEY_MOUSE: # its a mouse event
mouse_event = cur.getmouse() # so get the event data
if mouse_event[4] & cur.BUTTON_CLICKED: # and test event type
   # Do some thing with the BUTTON1 event
```

A complete but minimal mouse-enabled program follows.

Example 11.1 Minimal Mouse example

```
import curses as cur

# define mouse event indices
BSTATE = 4

def main(scr):
    # initialize mouse handling
    msk, _ = cur.mousemask(cur.ALL_MOUSE_EVENTS)

    scr.addstr("Click the mouse to see what happens," +
               " Q to quit")
    scr.refresh()
    count = 0

    # start event loop
    while True:
       ch = scr.getch()
       scr.clear()
       if ch in (ord('q'), ord('Q')):
          break
       # Handle mouse events
       if ch == cur.KEY_MOUSE:
          mev = cur.getmouse()
          count += 1
          scr.addstr(2,0, "Mouse event %d detected" % count)
          if mev[BSTATE] & cur.BUTTON1_CLICKED:
             scr.addstr(3,0, "Pressed button 1")
       scr.addstr(0,0,
                  "Click the mouse to see what happens" +
                  " Q to quit")
       scr.refresh()

cur.wrapper(main)
```

Putting it all Together

That's pretty much all there is to interfacing with a mouse. Let's create the same menu as we did in chapter 11 but this time use the mouse to select a menu option. To make things simpler, key handling has been removed.

Example 11.2 Access the menu with mouse!

```
import curses as cur
# define global constants
X = 1
Y = 2
BSTATE = -1
WIDTH=30
HEIGHT=10
choices = [
  "Choice 1",
  "Choice 2",
  "Choice 3",
  "Choice 4",
  "Exit",
]
n_choices = len(choices)

def print_menu(m_win):
   x = 2
   y = 2
   m_win.box()
   for n,choice in enumerate(choices):
       m_win.addstr(y+n, x, choice)
   m_win.refresh()

# determine if mouse click is inside window
def in_window(win, event):
   y,x = win.getbegyx() # get window origin
   h,w = win.getmaxyx() # get window height/width
   return (event[Y] >= y + 2 and
           event[Y] <= y + n_choices + 1 and
```

```
            event[X] >= x + 2 and
            event[X] <= x + w -1)

# get the choices index the user clicked on
def report_choice(win,event):
   y,x = win.getbegyx()
   y += 2              # account for borders & margins
   for n,_ in enumerate(choices):
      if event[Y]-y == n: # we pressed on this item
         break
   if n == n_choices-1: return -1
   else: return n

def main(scr):
   cur.curs_set(0)         # make cursor invisible
   scr.clear()

   # Try to put the window in the middle of screen
   choice = 0
   choice_fmt = "Choice made is : %d String Chosen is '%10s'"
   startx = (cur.COLS - WIDTH) // 2
   starty = (cur.LINES - HEIGHT) // 2
   scr.addstr(cur.LINES-1, 1, "Click on Exit to quit")
   scr.refresh()

   # Print the menu for the first time
   menu_win = cur.newwin(HEIGHT, WIDTH, starty, startx)
   menu_win.keypad(True) # receive mouse events in window
   print_menu(menu_win)

   # Get all the mouse events
   cur.mousemask(cur.ALL_MOUSE_EVENTS)

   while True:
      c = menu_win.getch()
      if c in [ord('q'),ord('Q')]:
         break
      if c == cur.KEY_MOUSE:
         event = cur.getmouse()
         # When user clicks left mouse button in the menu box
```

```
        if ( (event[BSTATE] & cur.BUTTON1_CLICKED) and
              in_window(menu_win,event) ):
           choice = report_choice(menu_win, event)
           if choice == -1:    # Exit chosen
              break
           else:
              scr.addstr(cur.LINES-5, 1,
                  choice_fmt % (choice, choices[choice]))
              scr.refresh()
     print_menu(menu_win)

cur.wrapper(main)
```

Most of this should look familiar. The main complication is the code that determines which item has been clicked. The problem is that the mouse coordinates are screen-based not window based (even though the `keypad()` function that turns on mouse event detection is window based!). This means that we need to get the menu's screen coordinates then do the necessary arithmetic to calculate whether the mouse is inside the menu and if so which item is being chosen. The `in_window()` and `report_choice()` functions take care of that.

I'll leave it as an exercise for the reader to combine examples 11.1 and 12.2 to handle both mouse and key navigation.

mouseinterval()

The `curses.mouseinterval()` function sets the maximum time (in milliseconds) that can elapse between press and release events in order for them to be recognized as a click. This function returns the previous interval value. The default is 200ms.

ungetmouse()

This function does the opposite of `getmouse()` in that it pushes an event back onto the event queue. Note that it operates at the curses level not the window.

```
curses.ungetmouse(id,x,y,z,bstate)
```

This can be used to push back an existing event or even to push a new artificial mouse event onto the queue for later processing. These are rarely used in practice but occasionally can be useful.

The Mouse Wheel

The mouse wheel found on some mice is supported by curses. In the C ncurses library the rotation of the wheel forward is reported as a `BUTTON4_PRESSED` event and the reverse rotation as `BUTTON5_PRESSED`. The first of these is defined in the Python curses module but unfortunately the `BUTTON5_PRESSED` event is not defined as a constant. It can still be detected but you will need to use its literal value (`0x200000` on my system) or define your own constants. For readability I prefer to define two new constants:

```
WHEEL_FORWARD = curses.BUTTON4_PRESSED
WHEEL_BACKWARD = 0x200000
```

12. Miscellaneous Features

At this point we have covered almost all the commonly used features of curses and you are equipped to write some sophisticated terminal-based user interfaces. However, there are a few extra features provided by curses that are worth mentioning but do not fit cleanly into any of the preceding chapters so we will consider them here.

Screen Dumping

While writing applications, especially games, sometimes it becomes necessary to store the state of the screen and restore it back to the same state later. It may even be the case that the restoration occurs much later, after the player has ended the program and then wants to restart where she left off. In C curses there is a function, `scr_dump()` that can be used to dump the screen contents to a file given as an argument. Later it can be restored by a `scr_restore()` function. Unfortunately these functions are not present in the Python implementation of curses, so we must do some extra work.

`putwin()` and `getwin()`

To store and restore windows, the methods `window.putwin(binfile)` and `curses.getwin(binfile)` can be used. `putwin()` puts the present window state into a file, opened in binary write mode, which can be later restored by `getwin()` using the same binary file in read mode. The `getwin()` method returns a window object, just like calling `curses.newwin()`

To save the whole screen we need to keep a list of the windows and then save each window in turn with a unique file name. To restore the screen we need to load each window file in turn. This technique is illustrated in the example below.

This is far from being a robust technique since adding new files could corrupt the scheme, a more foolproof technique would be to add the saved files to an archive such as a zip file. We could then unzip the file and load the files contained therein. Things get even more complicated when derived or sub-windows are used, the window list needs to take account of these nested hierarchies and the restoration needs to recreate them.

Example 12.1 Save/restore screen demonstration

```
import curses as cur
import os

def save_windows(winlist, path="/tmp"):
    for num,win in enumerate(winlist):
        fname = path+"/win"+str(num)+".cur"
        with open(fname,'wb') as f:
            win.putwin(f)

def restore_windows(path="/tmp"):
    files = [f for f in os.listdir(path)
                if f.endswith('.cur')]
    files.sort()
    windows = []
    for f in files:
        fn = os.path.join(path,f)
        win = cur.getwin(open(fn, 'rb'))
        windows.append(win)
    return windows

def main(scr):
    # set up screen and initialise colors
    cur.init_pair(1, cur.COLOR_BLUE,cur.COLOR_YELLOW)
```

```
    cur.init_pair(2, cur.COLOR_WHITE, cur.COLOR_BLUE)
    cur.init_pair(3, cur.COLOR_BLACK, cur.COLOR_RED)
    scr.bkgd(' ', cur.color_pair(1))
    scr.refresh()

    # create 2 new colored windows
    win1 = cur.newwin(3,10,cur.LINES//4,cur.COLS//4)
    win1.bkgd(' ',cur.color_pair(2))
    win1.box()
    win1.refresh()

    win2 = cur.newwin(3,10,cur.LINES//4,(cur.COLS//4)+30)
    win2.bkgd('.',cur.color_pair(3))
    win2.box()
    win2.refresh()

    # save this screen configuration as our "home screen"
    save_windows([scr,win1,win2])

    # now clear screen and reset colors
    scr.addstr(cur.LINES-2,1, "Hit a key to clear...")
    scr.getch()
    scr.clear()
    scr.bkgd(' ',cur.A_NORMAL)
    scr.getch()

    # now restore the home screen
    wins = restore_windows()
    for win in wins:
       win.refresh()

    wins[0].addstr(20,2,"Hit enter to exit...")
    wins[0].refresh()

    scr.getch()

cur.wrapper(main)
```

Note that we created two new functions to save and restore the windows and these used the `curses` module functions to do the work. We pass the list of windows to be saved (in the order in which they must be restored) and an optional path argument. The restore function reads all of the window files in the path and returns them as a list of window objects. We can then refresh each object to recreate the original screen at the time of saving. This is, of course, a simplistic example relying on the numbering of the windows to control sequence. That would fail if there were more than 10 windows, in which case a more robust file naming scheme would need to be designed. Similarly using `/tmp` as a save folder is only useful for short-term storage; a dedicated project folder (or zip file) would be safer.

Note that this facility only saves and restores the screen not the application data. You need to recreate the data yourself, possibly by saving/restoring them using standard Python techniques such as the `pickle` or `shelve` modules or a database.

curs_set()

This function can be used to make the cursor invisible. The parameter to this function should be `0` : invisible or `1` : normal or `2` : very visible (usually bold).

This is sometimes useful for games where you want to move windows around on screen without an obvious cursor to distract the user.

Temporarily Leaving Curses Mode

Sometimes you may want to get back to non-curses mode temporarily, perhaps to call a function that has `print()` statements embedded or even to launch an OS shell tool that displays output on screen. In such a case you will first need to tell curses to store the tty modes with a call to `def_prog_mode()` and then call `endwin()` to end the curses mode. This will leave you in the original tty mode.

To get back to curses once you are done, call `reset_prog_mode()`. This function returns the tty to the state stored by `def_prog_mode()`. Then do `refresh()`, and you are back to the curses mode. Note that you do not need to call `initscr()` a second time. Here is an example showing the sequence of things to be done.

Example 12.2. Temporarily Leaving Curses Mode

```
import curses as cur
import os, time

def main(scr):
   scr.addstr("Hit return to leave curses", cur.A_REVERSE)
   scr.getch()

   cur.def_prog_mode() # Save the tty modes
   cur.endwin() # End curses mode temporarily

   # Use the normal Python commands for input/output etc
   # ensure terminal restored fully
   os.system("clear; stty echo -nl")
   print("Back in terminal mode")
   time.sleep(1)
   input("Hit return to go back to curses")

   # Now go back into our curses screen
   cur.reset_prog_mode() # Return to the previous tty mode
   scr.refresh()         # restore the Screen contents
```

```
    scr.addstr(1,1,"Welcome back!", cur.A_UNDERLINE)

    scr.addstr(22,0,"Hit a key to exit...")
    scr.getch()

cur.wrapper(main)
```

Note that there is an equivalent pair of functions `def_shell_mode()` and `reset_shell_mode()` that can be used in a similar fashion but from the shell side. In practice, the prog_mode versions will usually be more useful.

ACS_ Variables

If you have ever programmed in DOS, you know about those nifty characters in the extended character set. They are printable only on some terminals. Curses functions like `box()` use these characters. All these variables start with ACS meaning Alternative Character Set. You might have noticed me using these characters in some of the programs above. Here's an example showing some of the ACS characters. The full list is detailed in the Python curses documentation.

Example 12.3 ACS Variables Example

```
import curses as cur

scr = cur.initscr()
scr.addstr("Upper left corner \t")
scr.addch(cur.ACS_ULCORNER)
scr.addstr("\n\nLower left corner \t")
scr.addch(cur.ACS_LLCORNER)
scr.addstr("\n\nLower right corner \t")
scr.addch(cur.ACS_LRCORNER)
scr.addstr("\n\nTee pointing right \t")
scr.addch(cur.ACS_LTEE)
scr.addstr("\n\nTee pointing left \t")
scr.addch(cur.ACS_RTEE)
```

```
scr.addstr("\n\nTee pointing up \t")
scr.addch(cur.ACS_BTEE)
scr.addstr("\n\nHit a key to exit...")

scr.getch()
cur.endwin()
```

And finally...

There are a number of other functions and methods in the `curses` module. Many of them are used to find out information about the terminal capabilities by querying the terminfo database. Some are related to old serial terminal characteristics that don't apply with terminal emulators. Others handle so called "wide characters". Still others control graphics and the refresh mechanism. These are outside the scope of this tutorial but are described in the `curses` module documentation.

The following table lists the functions that we have not covered in this book, they are all covered in the curses module documentation:

curses functions

`baudrate()`	`beep()`	`delay_output()`
`erasechar()`	`filter()`	`flash()`
`flushinp()`	`getsyx()`	`has_ic()`
`has_il()`	`has_key()`	`is_term_resized()`
`isendwin()`	`keyname()`	`killchar()`
`longname()`	`meta()`	`nl()`
`nonl()`	`noqiflush()`	`qiflush()`
`resetty()`	`resizeterm()`	`savetty()`
`get_escdelay()`	`set_escdelay()`	`get_tabsize()`
`set_tabsize()`	`setsyx()`	`termattrs()`
`termname()`	`tigetflag()`	`tigetnum()`
`tparm()`	`typeahead()`	`unctrl()`
`ungetch()`	`update_lines_cols()`	`unget_wch()`
`use_env()`	`use_default()`	

Window methods

clearok()	cursyncup()	echochar()
enclose()	encode()	erase()
get_wch()	idcok()	idlok()
immedok()	insdelln()	is_linetouched()
is_wintouched()	leaveok()	noutrefresh()
overlay()	overwrite()	redrawln()
redrawwin()	setscrreg()	standend()
standout()	syncdown()	syncok()
syncup()	timeout()	touchline()

13. The `curses.panel` module

While curses is capable of producing sophisticated user interfaces complete with multiple windows, menus and other widgets, it is not easy to manage all of these on screen at once. It is very easy to get the refresh order wrong or to discover that one window is obscuring some critical part of another. That's the problem that the `curses.panel` module is designed to solve, or at least to bring some semblance of order.

If you think of the application windows as being like pieces of paper lying on a desk over-lapping each other, that's called the stack. The fundamental difficulty is that you need to refresh your windows from the bottom of the stack upwards. The panel module assists in this by building and maintaining the stack order. You can pop a window to the top of the stack to make it visible and `panel` will ensure the lower windows are all kept in their right places in the stack.

Panel Basics

A panel object is a kind of window that is implicitly treated as part of a stack of panel objects. The top panel is completely visible and the lower panels' visibility depends on how much the higher panels hide them. There is a Panel method called `update_panels()` which, when called, displays all the panels in the stack in the correct order. You can think of it as being similar to the `window refresh()` method but for a stack of panels rather than a single window.

Each panel has an associated window object plus a general purpose data field called `userptr`, which is accessed via `set_userptr()` and `userptr()` panel methods. Any kind of Python object can be associated with this field. (The name is a nod to curses' C origins where a pointer type is simply a memory address.)

Other methods are provided to `hide()` or `show()` or `move()` individual panels. You can also bring a panel to the `top()` or `bottom()` of the stack as well as locate the panel immediately `above()` or `below()` the current panel.

The overlapping problem is managed by the `panel` library during all the calls to these methods.

The general flow of a panel program goes like this:

- Create the windows to be attached to the panels using the usual `curses.newwin()` function.
- Create panels with the `panel.new_panel()` function, passing an associated window object. It helps to create the panels in the desired visibility order although you can, of course, modify this later. The first panel will be at the bottom of the stack. You need to keep an explicit reference to each panel or the garbage collector will promptly destroy it again!
- Call `panel.update_panels()` to write the panels to the virtual screen in correct visibility order. Follow that with a `curses.doupdate()` to show it on the screen.
- Manipulate the panels with `panel.show()`, `panel.hide()`, `panel.move()`. Use helper methods like `panel.hidden() and panel.window()`. Make use of the `userptr` to store custom data.
- When you are done with the panel use the regular Python `del()` to delete the panel if necessary.

Let's make the concepts clear with some programs. The following is a simple program which creates 3 overlapping panels and shows them on the screen.

Example 13.1 Panel basics

```
import curses as cur
import curses.panel as pan

def main(scr):
   lines = 10
   cols = 40
   y = 2
   x = 4
   my_wins = []
   my_panels = []

   cur.start_color()
   cur.init_pair(1, cur.COLOR_WHITE,cur.COLOR_RED)
   cur.init_pair(2, cur.COLOR_BLUE,cur.COLOR_YELLOW)
   cur.init_pair(3, cur.COLOR_BLACK,cur.COLOR_GREEN)

   # Create overlapping windows for the panels
   my_wins.append(cur.newwin(lines, cols, y, x))
   my_wins.append(cur.newwin(lines, cols, y+1, x+5))
   my_wins.append(cur.newwin(lines, cols, y+2, x+10))

   # Create borders around windows to see the effect
   for win in my_wins:
       win.box()

   # Attach a panel to each window - order bottom up
   my_panels.append(pan.new_panel(my_wins[0]))
   my_panels.append(pan.new_panel(my_wins[1]))
   my_panels.append(pan.new_panel(my_wins[2]))
   # order is now: stdscr-0-1-2

   # write some identifying text
   my_wins[0].addstr(1,1,"Window 1",cur.color_pair(1))
   my_wins[1].addstr(1,1,"Window 2",cur.color_pair(2))
   my_wins[2].addstr(1,1,"Window 3",cur.color_pair(3))

   pan.update_panels()
   cur.doupdate()     # Show it on the screen
```

```
    scr.getch() # pause…

    # bring panel 2 to top and write a message
    my_panels[1].top()
    my_panels[1].window().addstr(3,2, "Msg via panel")

    pan.update_panels()
    cur.doupdate()
    scr.getch()

cur.wrapper(main)
```

As you can see, the program follows the simple flow as explained above. The windows are created with `curses.newwin()` and then they are attached to panels with `panel.new_panel()`. As we attach one panel after another, the stack of panels gets updated. To put them on screen `panel.update_panels()` and `curses.doupdate()` are called. We then use the `top()` method of panel 2 to bring it to the top and the `window()` method to access the attached window object so that we can call `addstr()`. We then repeat the update dance to display the result.

Panel Window Browsing

A slightly more complex example is given below. This program creates 3 windows which can be cycled through using the tab key. Have a look at the code.

Example 13.2. Panel Window Browsing Example

```
import curses as cur

import curses.panel as pan

from curses.ascii import ESC


NLINES=10

NCOLS=40
```

```
KEY_TAB = 9    # define a new Key constant


def main(scr):
   my_panels = []
   scr.keypad(True)

   # Initialize all the colors
   cur.start_color()
   cur.init_pair(1, cur.COLOR_RED, cur.COLOR_BLACK)
   cur.init_pair(2, cur.COLOR_GREEN, cur.COLOR_BLACK)
   cur.init_pair(3, cur.COLOR_BLUE, cur.COLOR_BLACK)
   cur.init_pair(4, cur.COLOR_CYAN, cur.COLOR_BLACK)

   my_wins = init_wins(3)

   # Attach a panel to each window, Order is bottom up
   my_panels.append(pan.new_panel(my_wins[0]))
   my_panels.append(pan.new_panel(my_wins[1]))
   my_panels.append(pan.new_panel(my_wins[2]))

   # Show instructions on the screen
   scr.attron(cur.color_pair(4))
   scr.addstr(cur.LINES-3, 1,
            "Use tab to browse through the windows\n" +
           "or number(1-3) to bring to top. (ESC to Exit)")
   scr.attroff(cur.color_pair(4))
   pan.update_panels()
   cur.doupdate()
```

```
# start event loop
   while True:
      top = pan.top_panel()
      ch = scr.getch()
      if ch == cur.ESC:
         break   # exit event loop
      if ch == KEY_TAB:
         top.bottom()
      if chr(ch) in ('1','2','3'):
         my_panels[int(chr(ch))-1].top()
      pan.update_panels()
      cur.doupdate()

# Create all the windows
def init_wins(n_wins):
   y = 2
   x = 10
   wins = []
   for n in range(n_wins):
      win = cur.newwin(NLINES, NCOLS, y+(3*n), x+(7*n))
      lbl = "Window Number %d" % (n+1)
      win_show(win, lbl, n+1)
      wins.append(win)
   return wins

# Show the window with a border and a label
def win_show(win, label, label_color):
   starty,startx = win.getbegyx()
   height,width = win.getmaxyx()
   win.box()
```

```
    win.addch(2, 0, cur.ACS_LTEE)
    win.hline(2, 1, cur.ACS_HLINE, width-2)
    win.addch(2, width-1, cur.ACS_RTEE)
    print_in_middle(win,1,label, cur.color_pair(label_color))

# Print label in middle of line
def print_in_middle(win, line, label, col_pair):
    _,width = win.getmaxyx()
    length = len(label)
    x = (width-length) // 2
    win.addstr(line, x, label, col_pair)
    win.refresh()

cur.wrapper(main)
```

This is essentially the same as the last example except I've made the individual windows a bit flashier with the addition of a title bar. This allows me to demonstrate the use of the ACS characters we discussed earlier. The main loop should by now look familiar and the only points of note are the use of the `bottom()` and `top()` methods to manipulate the panel stack and the `panel.top_panel()` function to get a reference to the current top panel.

The `win_show()` function simply draws the border and title bar area to the window and adds the title by calling `print_in_middle()`. I've tried to make these fairly generic so that you can easily extend the example by adding more windows should you wish to experiment. We also reuse them in the remaining examples in this chapter.

Moving and Resizing Panels

The function `move_panel()` moves a panel to the desired location on the screen. It doesn't change the stack in any way. Be sure to use `move_panel()` rather than `mvwin()` on the window associated with the panel.

Resizing a panel is slightly complex because there is no resize method. One solution is to create a new window as a duplicate of the old window but with the new sizes. You can then change the window associated with the panel using `replace()`. Don't forget to delete the old window. The window associated with a panel can be found by using the `panel.window()` method as seen in the first example. Obviously if the window is complex with many fields and sub-windows etc. then creating and resizing a clone may be difficult.

The following program shows these concepts in practice. You can cycle through the panels with <TAB> as before. To resize or move the active panel press 'r' for resize 'm' for moving. Then use the arrow keys to resize or move it as required, finally pressing enter to end your resizing or moving. (Note the window does not move or resize in real time on the screen, you need to hit Enter to see the change.) This example makes use of a user defined class `Panel_Data` to hold the data required for the operations and stores it in the `userptr` field. It is quite a long example but you have seen the majority of it before in the earlier examples. The important thing is to focus on the event loop and how the various events are handled.

Example 13.3. Panel Moving and Resizing example

```
import curses as cur
import curses.panel as pan
from curses.ascii import ESC

class Panel_Data:   # data record for panel userptr
  def __init__(self, x, y, w, h, label, color):
    self.x = x
    self.y = y
    self.w = w
```

```
        self.h = h
        self.label = label
        self.color = color


NLINES = 10
NCOLS = 40
KEY_TAB = ord('\t')
KEY_RETURN = ord('\n')

def main(scr):
    resize,move = False,False

    # Initialize all the colors
    cur.init_pair(1, cur.COLOR_RED, cur.COLOR_BLACK)
    cur.init_pair(2, cur.COLOR_GREEN, cur.COLOR_BLACK)
    cur.init_pair(3, cur.COLOR_BLUE, cur.COLOR_BLACK)
    cur.init_pair(4, cur.COLOR_CYAN, cur.COLOR_BLACK)
    cur.init_pair(5, cur.COLOR_YELLOW, cur.COLOR_BLACK)

    # Attach a panel to each window. Order is bottom up
    my_wins = init_wins(4) # create 4 windows
    my_panels = []
    for w in my_wins:
        my_panels.append(pan.new_panel(w))
        set_user_ptrs(my_panels)

    # Show it on the screen
    scr.attron(cur.color_pair(5))
    scr.addstr(cur.LINES-3, 0,
               "Use 'm' for moving, 'r' for resizing")
    scr.addstr(cur.LINES-2, 0,
               "Use tab to select window (ESC to Exit)")
    pan.update_panels()  # update virtual screen
    cur.doupdate()       # show on physical screen

    # start event loop
    while True:
        stack_top = pan.top_panel()
        top_data = stack_top.userptr()
```

```
ch = scr.getch()
if ch == ESC:      # exit
   break
if ch == KEY_TAB:  # switch window
   stack_top.bottom()
elif ch == ord('r'):   # Re-Size
   resize = True
   scr.addstr(cur.LINES-4, 0,
       "Entered Resizing: Use Arrows to resize," +
       " <ENTER> to end")
   scr.refresh()
elif ch == ord('m'):   # Move
   move = True
   scr.addstr(cur.LINES-4, 0,
      "Entered Moving: Use Arrows to Move," +
      " <ENTER> to end")
   scr.refresh()
elif ch == cur.KEY_LEFT:
   if resize:
      top_data.w += 1
      resize_pane(stack_top)
   if move:
      top_data.x -= 1
      move_pane(stack_top)
elif ch == cur.KEY_RIGHT:
   if resize:
      top_data.w -= 1
      resize_pane(stack_top)
   if move:
      top_data.x += 1
      move_pane(stack_top)
elif ch == cur.KEY_UP:
   if resize:
      top_data.h += 1
      resize_pane(stack_top)
   if move:
      top_data.y -= 1
      move_pane(stack_top)
elif ch == cur.KEY_DOWN:
   if resize:
```

```
            top_data.h -= 1
            resize_pane(stack_top)
         if move:
            top_data.y += 1
            move_pane(stack_top)
      elif ch == KEY_RETURN:        # End move/resize modes
         scr.move(cur.LINES-4, 0)  # remove message
         scr.clrtoeol()
         scr.refresh()
         if resize:
            resize = False
         if move:
            move = False

      # end of events, so update screen
      pan.update_panels()
      cur.doupdate()

# Set the userptr data for individual panels
def set_user_ptrs(panels):
   ptrs = []
   for n,panel in enumerate(panels):
       w = panel.window()
       y,x = w.getbegyx()
       h,w = w.getmaxyx()
       data = Panel_Data(x,y,w,h,
                        "Window Number %d" % (n+1), n+1)
       panel.set_userptr(data)

def resize_pane(fm):
    data = fm.userptr()
    try:
        fmw = cur.newwin(data.h,data.w,data.y,data.x)
        win_show(fmw, data.label,data.color)
        fm.replace(fmw)
    except cur.error: pass

def move_pane(fm):
    data = fm.userptr()
    try: fm.move(data.y,data.x)
```

```
    except pan.error: pass

# Create all the windows
def init_wins(n_wins):
    y = 2
    x = 10
    wins = []
    for n in range(n_wins):
       win = cur.newwin(NLINES, NCOLS, y+(3*n), x+(7*n))
       lbl = "Window Number %d" % (n+1)
       win_show(win, lbl, n+1)
       wins.append(win)
    return wins

# Show the window with a border and a label
def win_show(win, label, label_color):
   starty,startx = win.getbegyx()
   height,width = win.getmaxyx()
   win.box()
   win.addch(2, 0, cur.ACS_LTEE)
   win.hline(2, 1, cur.ACS_HLINE, width-2)
   win.addch(2, width-1, cur.ACS_RTEE)
   print_in_middle(win, 1, label,
                   cur.color_pair(label_color))
   win.refresh()

def print_in_middle(win, line, label, col_pair):
   _,width = win.getmaxyx()
   length = len(label)
   x = (width-length) // 2
   win.addstr(line, x, label, col_pair)
   win.refresh()

cur.wrapper(main)
```

OK, That is a long example but focus your attention on the event loop and event handlers.

ESC signals the end of the program.

TAB cycles through the panels by sending the currently top panel to the bottom.

If 'r' is pressed resizing mode is started and a help message displayed. After this the new sizes are updated in the selected panel's `userptr` object as the user presses the arrow keys. The resize occurs by creating a new window using the updated `userptr` data and then replacing the old window with the new one. If the panel is made too small a `curses.error` occurs and is caught but ignored. (We could print a warning message to the user instead, but we'd need to remove it again later.) When the user eventually presses `<ENTER>` resize mode is turned off and the help text removed.

When the user presses 'm' the move mode starts and the help message is displayed. This is much simpler than resizing since there is a `move()` panel method that we can use. As the arrow keys are pressed the new position is updated in the `userptr` data and the move operation uses the new data. If the panel is moved off screen a `panel.error` occurs this time, which again we ignore. Pressing `<ENTER>` ends move mode and removes the help text.

In this program the user data which is stored in the `Panel_Data` objects, plays an important role in keeping the associated information with a panel. The `Panel_Data` stores the panel coordinates, sizes, label, and label colour which are all passed to the `win_show()` function. The geometry data is also used by the resize and move functions.

One small point to note is that in this program we defined the `KEY_TAB` and `KEY_RETURN` constants by using the `ord()` function rather than using literal numbers. This helps to make the code just a bit more portable between systems.

Hiding and Showing Panels

A panel can be hidden, or made invisible, by using the `Panel.hide()` method. This method merely removes it from the stack of panels, thus hiding it on the screen after you do `panel.update_panels()`. It can be shown again by using the `Panel.show()` method.

The following program demonstrates hiding and showing of panels. Press the number of the window to toggle its visibility. The `panel.hidden()` method tests whether a panel is currently hidden or not.

Example 13.4. Panel Hiding and Showing example

```
import curses as cur
import curses.panel as pan
from curses.ascii import ESC

NLINES = 10
NCOLS = 40

def main(scr):
   # Initialize all the colors
   cur.init_pair(1, cur.COLOR_RED, cur.COLOR_BLACK)
   cur.init_pair(2, cur.COLOR_GREEN, cur.COLOR_BLACK)
   cur.init_pair(3, cur.COLOR_BLUE, cur.COLOR_BLACK)
   cur.init_pair(4, cur.COLOR_CYAN, cur.COLOR_BLACK)

   # Attach a panel to each window. Set all visible
   my_wins = init_wins(4) # create 4 wndows
   my_panels = [pan.new_panel(w) for w in my_wins]
   # Show it on the screen
   scr.attron(cur.color_pair(4))
   scr.addstr(cur.LINES-3, 0,
              "Use '1-4' to toggle visibility")
   scr.addstr(cur.LINES-2, 0, "ESC to Exit")
   pan.update_panels()
   cur.doupdate()
```

```
    # Start event loop
    while True:
        ch = scr.getch()
        if ch == ESC:
            break
        if ch in [ord('1'), ord('2'), ord('3'), ord('4')]:
            index = int(chr(ch)) - 1 # zero index!
            thePanel = my_panels[index]
            if thePanel.hidden():
                thePanel.show()
            else:
                thePanel.hide()
        pan.update_panels()
        cur.doupdate()

# Create all the windows
def init_wins(n_wins):
    y = 2
    x = 10
    wins = []
    for n in range(n_wins):
        win = cur.newwin(NLINES, NCOLS, y+(3*n), x+(7*n))
        lbl = "Window Number %d" % (n+1)
        win_show(win, lbl, n+1)
        wins.append(win)
    return wins

# Show the window with a border and a label
def win_show(win, label, label_color):
    starty,startx = win.getbegyx()
    height,width = win.getmaxyx()
    win.box()
    win.addch(2, 0, cur.ACS_LTEE)
    win.hline(2, 1, cur.ACS_HLINE, width-2)
    win.addch(2, width-1, cur.ACS_RTEE)
    print_in_middle(win, 1, label,
                    cur.color_pair(label_color))
    win.refresh()
```

```
def print_in_middle(win, line, label, col_pair):
    _,width = win.getmaxyx()
    length = len(label)
    x = (width-length) // 2
    win.addstr(line, x, label, col_pair)
    win.refresh()

cur.wrapper(main)
```

Again, all the significant code is in the event loop. The rest is virtually identical to the previous example. We use the `hidden()`, `hide()` and `show()` methods to toggle the state of the selected panel.

14. Tools and Widget Libraries

You have now covered almost everything that the Python standard library offers for writing curses programs. There is one bonus component that we will discuss next. However, in the wider Python ecosystem you will also find third party modules that extend curses in various ways. In the C world there are many more but these are not generally available for Python. A search of the PyPi repository may throw up exactly what you need (https://pypi.org/).

In this chapter we consider one additional module that, while not specifically designed to work in curses, does offer a comprehensive set of GUI style dialog boxes for use in terminal applications. This is called the `dialog` module and is a wrapper around a C tool of the same name (which is based on curses).

Finally I briefly discuss a more modern framework for building terminal applications that is built on top of curses but feels more like a traditional GUI framework, it's called `urwid`.

But first we look at our bonus component, the `textpad`.

curses.textpad

`curses.textpad` contains a text editor widget, `Textbox`, that supports the basic emacs keystrokes (Ctrl-a for start of line, Ctrl-k for delete to end of line, etc.) It also supports the cursor movement arrow keys, etc. This section provides a basic example of its use.

<u>Example 14.1 curses.textpad example</u>

```
import curses as cur
from curses.textpad import Textbox

def main(scr):
   s = "Here is a string to insert..."
   scr.addstr(0,0,"Edit the text then hit Ctrl-G to exit")
   scr.refresh()

   # create the text box with border around the outside.
   tb_border = cur.newwin(12,52,4,4)
   tb_border.box()
   tb_border.refresh()
   tb_body = cur.newwin(10,50,5,5)
   tb = Textbox(tb_body)

   for ch in s:          # insert the starting text
      tb.do_command(ch)
   tb.edit()          # start the editor running, Ctrl-G ends
   s2 = tb.gather()     # fetch the contents
   scr.clear()          # clear the screen
   scr.addstr(0,0,"The text in the box was:\n")
   scr.addstr(3,0,s2)  # display edited contents of textbox
   scr.refresh()
   scr.getch()


cur.wrapper(main)
```

Note that by default the textbox has no border, you need to create a window one row and one column larger all round and add the border there. To enter text into the text box you call the `do_command()` method passing in the command string. A single character is treated as input data. You can also pass navigation and other commands to operate the editor programmatically, but usually you just want to pass control to the user. Finally, you can read the contents of the editor with the `gather()` method which returns the entire contents as a string.

dialog

The `dialog` command is a Linux tool for creating professional looking dialog boxes in terminal applications. It is a command-line tool intended to be used in shell scripts. There is however a Python wrapper module making this capability available to Python programs and the good news for us is that it is curses compatible. The dialog command man page has all the details but we will take a look at the basics here.

You need `dialog` to be installed on your OS, but most Linux systems include it. The Python module can then be installed from the Python Package Index (PyPI) with

```
$ python3 -m pip install pythondialog
```

A simple example showing a curses program displaying a message using dialog follows.

Example 14.2 curses and dialog example

```
import curses as cur
import dialog


def main(scr):
   d = dialog.Dialog() # initialize dialog
```

```
    # use curses to get the input.
    cur.echo() # show the input as typed
    scr.addstr(3,3,"Hello, what's your name? ")
    nm = scr.getstr()

    # use dialog to display the name
    d.msgbox("Hi %s, nice to meet you." % nm.decode('utf-8'))
    # go back to curses to clear up
    scr.clear()
    scr.addstr("\nGoodbye")
    scr.refresh()
    cur.napms(1000)

cur.wrapper(main)
```

The dialog system includes over 20 different widgets including file browsers, menus, progress gauges, text browsers, calendars and more. The web page provides a tutorial and complete reference:

http://pythondialog.sourceforge.net/doc/index.html

urwid

Urwid is a third party application framework for building terminal applications. It is best suited to form-like user interfaces with menus, data fields, labels, buttons, etc. It is a comprehensive framework and cannot be easily mixed with regular curses so it's best thought of as something completely separate and with its own (fairly steep) learning curve.

The following is a basic "Hello World" type program as shown in the urwid tutorial, just to give a hint of how an urwid program looks.

Example 14.3 Urwid framework example

```
import urwid

def show_or_exit(key):
   if key in ('q', 'Q'):
      raise urwid.ExitMainLoop()
   txt.set_text(repr(key))

txt = urwid.Text(u"Hello World")
fill = urwid.Filler(txt, 'top')
loop = urwid.MainLoop(fill, unhandled_input=show_or_exit)
loop.run()
```

Urwid can be found at http://urwid.org and can be installed using pip with

```
python -m pip install urwid
```

15. A Case Study – The Totalizer

So far we have used curses to build some short demonstration programs. In this chapter I want to look at a more real-world type of project using curses as the display mechanism but incorporating it into an object-oriented application, typical of the sort created for real users. We will build a mini spreadsheet-like application with a grid display of cells into which data can be entered and the total of the current column displayed. We will build it from a set of classes which are sufficiently general to be used for other types of grid based applications. It will incorporate some error checking although not to full industrial standards to save space. For the same reasons we will not write (or even discuss) unit tests such as would be used in a real project.

Totalizer Design Summary

The design for the Totalizer application is shown in Fig 1, as a simplified UML diagram.

The most basic class is the `Cell`, which simply holds a value and displays it. It also performs the valuable service of abstracting most of the low level curses code away from the higher level application classes. For instance, we can toggle inverse video on or off.

The next level of abstraction is a `Grid` component which uses a table structure of `Cells` and can, optionally, display headings for rows and columns. The clients can move the cursor to individual cells and store values into specified cells.

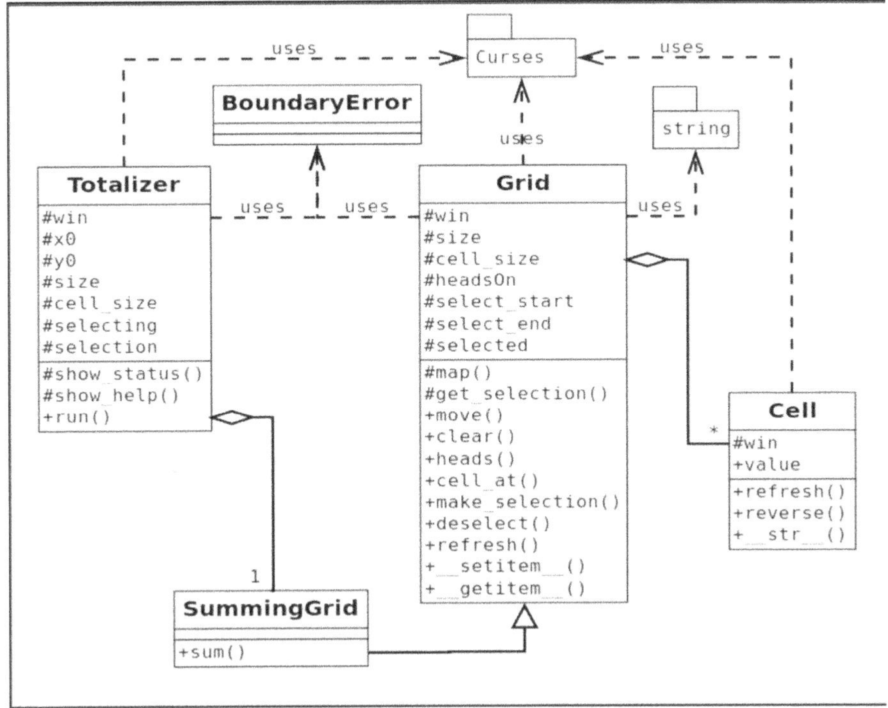

Figure 1 Totalizer UML class diagram

There is a specialization of the `Grid` called a `SummingGrid` which adds the ability to sum the column in which the cursor is currently located.

Finally, we have the `Totalizer` application class. This creates a `SummingGrid` and starts an event loop. It processes the navigation events and the data assignment, summation and exit commands.

Let's look at each of these classes in more detail.

The Cell Class

The `Cell` class is based on a `curses` sub-window. It stores the original data in a "private" field, `_value` which is exposed as a Python property, `value`. There is also a `refresh()` method which redraws the cell, including its border.

The public `reverse()` operation turns inverse video on or off for the cell.

Setting the cell value automatically updates the cell display. A `ValueError` is raised if the value is too big to fit the cell display. A `__str__()` operator is provided to simplify the display code.

The code is shown below:

```
import curses as cur

class Cell:
   def __init__(self, win, w,y,x, val=None):
     self.att = cur.A_NORMAL
     self.width = w
     self.isReversed = False
     self.theCell = win.subwin(3,w+2,y,x)
     self.theCell.box()
     self.value = val  # use setter to check validity
     self.refresh()

   @property
   def value(self): return self._value

   @value.setter
   def value(self,v):
     v = v if v else ''
     if len(str(v)) > self.width:
       raise ValueError("%d too large a value for cell"% v)
     self._value = v # actually store the value
     self.theCell.addstr(1,1,str(v).ljust(self.width))
```

```
    self.refresh() # now display it

  def reverse(self):
    if self.isReversed:
      self.att = cur.A_NORMAL
    else: cur.A_REVERSE
    self.isReversed = not self.isReversed
    self.refresh()

  def refresh(self):
    self.theCell.attrset(self.att)
    self.theCell.box()
    self.theCell.addstr(1,1,
                        str(self.value).ljust(self.width))
    self.theCell.refresh()

  def __str__(self):
    return str(self.value)
```

The Grid Class

The `Grid` is essentially a two dimensional array of `Cells`. In a sense it is like a bigger form of a curses window (which is an array of chars) and supports similar concepts.

The `move()` operation, like its curses counterpart, locates the cursor into a cell based on grid `y,x` coordinates. There is a private `_map()` method that converts the grid coordinates into underlying window coordinates so that the curses `move()` call ends up in the appropriate place. The coordinate values are checked for size and if outside the grid boundaries a bespoke `BoundaryError` is raised.

The `clear()` operation simply deletes the content of all cells and resets the cursor to the first cell.

The `heads()` operation turns on a spreadsheet-like header display with numbers along the top row and uppercase letters down the left most column, both displayed in inverse video. The application does not (currently!) use these letters and numbers for navigation; they are merely for the users convenience in locating specific cells. (There is also no way to turn off the display once turned on, a future version might add a Boolean parameter to indicate the desired state of the headers display.)

A `cell_at()` method translates the window coordinates into a grid cell coordinate-pair which can be used by the `move()` method. This is needed to handle mouse events.

The `make_selection()` and `deselect()` operations create and remove a highlighted selection area within the grid. A `get_selection()` private method returns a list of cells within the current selection.

Finally, we implement the `getitem/setitem` pair of operators to provide indexing into the grid. This allows clients to access cells as if using a table directly. We only implement a single index which returns a list of `Cells`. This list will handle the second index and the slicing operations needed for the `sum()` method. It is a convenience feature which hides the internal cell array.

The code is as follows:

```
import curses as cur
from cell import Cell
import string

class BoundaryError(ValueError): pass
```

```
class Grid:
   ''' Creates a grid of cells.
     Cells are accessed using grid rather than window
     coordinates. Allows movement to a cell, and reversing
     of display'''
   def __init__(self,win, h,w, y,x, cell_size=8):
     self.win = win
     self.headsOn = False
     self.selected = False
     self.select_start = None
     self.select_end = None
     self.size = (h,w)
     self.origin = (0,0) # initial origin with heads off
     self.yx = self.origin # initial active cell
     self.cell_size = cell_size
     self.cells = []
     for r in range(h): # generate empty grid
       row_y = y + (r*3)
       row = [Cell(win,cell_size, row_y, col*(cell_size+2)+x)
              for col in range(w)]
       self.cells.append(row)

   def _map(self,y,x): # helper function
   ''' Maps grid coords to window coords'''
     wy = 1 + (3*y)
     wx = 1 + (self.cell_size+2) * x
     return wy,wx

   def _get_selection(self):
   ''' Return a list of all cells currently selected'''
     if not self.selected:
        return []
     start_row,start_col = self.select_start
     end_row,end_col = self.select_end
     cells = []
     for row in range(start_row,end_row+1):
        for col in range(start_col,end_col+1):
          cells.append(self[row][col])
     return cells
```

```
def move(self,y,x):
''' Move cursor to cell y,x in grid'''
  if (y >= self.size[0] or    # check within boundaries
      x >= self.size[1] or
      y < self.origin[0] or
      x < self.origin[1]):
     raise BoundaryError("%d or %d outside grid"%(y,x))
  ypt,xpt = self._map(y,x)
  self.win.move(ypt,xpt)      # uses curses move()
  self.yx = (y,x)

def clear(self):
''' Clear all cells '''
  for row in self[self.origin[0]:]:
    for cell in row[self.origin[1]:]:
      cell.value = None
      cell.refresh()
  self.move(*self.origin)

def heads(self):
''' Insert numbers along row 0 and letters down col 0
    reverses cells in row 0 and column 0'''
  letters = string.ascii_uppercase
  for num,cell in enumerate(self.cells[0]):
    if num > 0:
      cell.value= str(num).center(self.cell_size)
    cell.reverse()
  for index,row in enumerate(self.cells[1:]):
    row[0].value = letters[index]
    row[0].reverse()
    for cell in row:
      cell.value = None
  self.headsOn = True
  self.origin = (1,1)
  self.move(*self.origin)

def cell_at(self, y,x):
''' Find cell with containing curses coords y,x.
    return grid y,x coordinates of cell '''
  row = y//3
```

```
    for row in self[self.origin[0]]:
      for cell in row:
        cell.value = None
    col = x//(self.cell_size+2)
    return row,col

  def make_selection(self,start,end):
  ''' Show selected cells in inverse video and set flag
      attributes'''
    self.selected = True
    self.select_start = start
    self.select_end = end
    for row in range(start[0],end[0]+1):
      for col in range(start[1],end[1]+1):
        self[row][col].reverse()
    if start == end:     # need to reinvert first cell
      self[start[0]][start[1]].reverse()

  def deselect(self):
  ''' Deselect the grid by reversing cells and resetting
     attributes'''
    for row in range(self.select_start[0],
                     self.select_end[0]+1):
       for col in range(self.select_start[1],
                        self.select_end[1]+1):
          self[row][col].reverse()
    self.selected = False
    self.select_start = None
    self.select_end = None

  def refresh(self):
  ''' Redraw the grid '''
    for row in self.cells:
      for cell in row:
        cell.refresh()

# allow access to cells via indexing of grid
  def __setitem__(self,index,cell):
    self.cells[index] = cell
```

```
def __getitem__(self,index):
  return self.cells[index]
```

The SummingGrid Class

The `SummingGrid` class is a simple subclass of `Grid`. It adds a single operation, `sum()`, which adds all the values in the current column which are not zero (or null) and returns the result. It takes account of whether headers exist or not. If a selection exists it returns the sum of all cells within the selection.

The code follows:

```
class SummingGrid(Grid):
   '''Adds ability to total a column to basic Grid'''

   def __init__(self,win,ht,wd,y,x, cell_size=8):
     super().__init__(win,ht,wd,y,x,cell_size)

   def sum(self,col):
   ''' Sums all values in current column'''
     first = 1 if self.headsOn else 0
     if self.selected:
       cells = self._get_selection()
       vals = [cell.value for cell in cells if cell.value]
     else:
       vals = [row[col].value for row in self[first:]
               if row[col].value]
     return sum(vals)
```

The Totalizer Class

The `Totalizer` is the application class. It creates a `SummingGrid` and turns on headers. Each cell displays itself as it is added and if it cannot fit into its window curses will raise an error. There is a convenience method, `show_status()`, for displaying messages on the bottom line of the window. The `show_help()` method displays a new window with help instructions. Any keypress or mouse click will close it and the grid will be refreshed. There is a single public operation: `run()`.

`run()` starts the event loop and processes the events. Allowed events include:

- F1, which pops up the help window.
- Arrow movements (or the vi editor key equivalents 'hjkl') to navigate the grid (complete with boundary checking).
- "=" an assignment operation comprised of the equals sign followed by a value, for example, typing "=42<RETURN>" will insert 42 into the current cell and move the cursor down to the next cell in the column.
- "+" which totals the current column (or selection if one is active), displaying the result as a status message.
- "C" which clears the contents of the grid.
- "S" which controls selection. The first "S" starts a selection and the chosen cell is highlighted. A second "S" marks the end of the selection and the range of cells is highlighted. Any addition operations while the selection is active will apply to the selection. A third "S" will deselect the region returning things to normal.
- "X" (or "x") exits the application.

Finally we handle mouse clicks to navigate to a new cell.

The code is as follows:

```
import curses as cur
from grid import Grid, BoundaryError

# define mouse event indices
X_COORD = 1
Y_COORD = 2
BUTTON_STATE = 4

class Totalizer:
   ''' Spreadsheet-like grid that can display totals of
      Columns. Values must be integers.'''
   help_string = "Press F1 (or H) for help, X to eXit."

   def __init__(self, win, ht,wd, cell_size=8):
     self.win = win
     self.size = (ht,wd)
     self.cell_size = cell_size
     self.selecting = False
     self.selection = None
     self.grid = SummingGrid(win,ht,wd, 0,0, cell_size)
     self.grid.heads()
     cur.mousemask(cur.ALL_MOUSE_EVENTS)

   def _show_status(self,msg):
   ''' Display message on bottom line of window '''
     Y,X = self.win.getmaxyx()
     y,x = self.grid.yx
     # clear line but not border
     self.win.addstr(Y-2,1, ' '*(X-2))
     self.win.addstr(Y-2,1, msg)
     self.grid.move(y,x)  # move cursor back to active cell

   def _show_help(self):
   '''Show help screen in new window, remove window on any
      key'''
     ht,wd = self.win.getmaxyx()
     top = (ht-15)//2
```

```
    left = (wd-50)//2
    win = cur.newwin(15,50,top,left)
    win.keypad(True)  # accept mouse clicks and special keys
    win.box()
    win.addstr(1,2,"Arrow keys move cursor")
    win.addstr(3,2,"Mouse positions cursor")
    win.addstr(5,2,"=N<RETURN> inserts value")
    win.addstr(7,2,"+ Sums the current column")
    win.addstr(9,2,"S Start/end/cancel selection")
    win.addstr(11,2,"C Clear grid")
    win.addstr(13,2,"X eXit the application")
    win.refresh()
    win.getch()  # any key or mouse click clears help screen
    win.erase()
    self.grid.refresh()
    # restore cursor to previous cell
    self.grid.move(*self.grid.yx)

  def run(self):
  ''' Start the event loop, process the actions '''
    Y,X = self.win.getmaxyx()
    self.win.addstr(Y-3,1, self.help_string)
    self.grid.move(*self.grid.origin) # starting position

    while True:
      key = self.win.getch()
      if key in [ord('X'),ord('x')]: break
      if key in [cur.KEY_F1,ord('H'),ord('h')]:
         self._show_help()
      elif key in [cur.KEY_UP, ord('k')]:
         y,x = self.grid.yx
         try: self.grid.move(y-1,x)
         except BoundaryError as e:
            self._show_status(e.args[0])
      elif key in [cur.KEY_DOWN, ord('j')]:
         y,x = self.grid.yx
         try: self.grid.move(y+1,x)
         except BoundaryError as e:
            self._show_status(e.args[0])
      elif key in [cur.KEY_LEFT, ord('h')]:
```

```
    y,x = self.grid.yx
    try: self.grid.move(y,x-1)
    except BoundaryError as e:
       self._show_status(e.args[0])
elif key in [cur.KEY_RIGHT, ord('l')]:
    y,x = self.grid.yx
    try: self.grid.move(y,x+1)
    except BoundaryError as e:
       self._show_status(e.args[0])
elif key == ord('='):
  val = self.win.getstr() # now read the data value
  y,x = self.grid.yx
  try:
    self.grid[y][x].value = int(val) # only integers
    self.grid.move(y+1,x)
  except BoundaryError: pass # leave it as-is
  except ValueError:
     self._show_status("Error: invalid value: %s" %
                       val)
elif key == ord('+'):
  y,x = self.grid.yx
  tot = self.grid.sum(x)
  self._show_status("Column %d total = %d" % (x,tot))
elif key == ord('S'):
  if not self.selecting and
     not self.selection:   # first S
     self.selecting = True
     self.selection = self.grid.yx
     # make selection of current cell
     self.grid.make_selection(self.selection,
                              self.selection)
     self._show_status("Selection ON")
  elif self.selecting:     # second S
     self.selecting = False
     self.grid.make_selection(self.selection,
                              self.grid.yx)
     self._show_status("Selection complete")
  else:                    # third S
     self.grid.deselect()
     self.selection = None
```

```
        self._show_status("Selection off")
    elif key == ord("C"):
      self.grid.clear()
    elif key == cur.KEY_MOUSE:
      m_event = cur.getmouse()
      if m_event[BUTTON_STATE] | cur.BUTTON1_CLICKED:
         m_y = m_event[Y_COORD]
         m_x = m_event[X_COORD]
         g_y,g_x = self.grid.cell_at(m_y,m_x)
         try: self.grid.move(g_y,g_x)
         except BoundaryError: pass     # leave it as-is
```

The Driver Code

Finally, the driver code for the application in the `main()` function is called by the `curses.wrapper()`. It draws a box around `stdscr`, calculates how many cells we can fit on the screen (taking account of cell borders etc), then creates a `Totalizer`.

Finally the event loop is started by sending the `run()` message to the instance.

The code is inserted at the end of the totalizer.py file as follows:

```
import curses as cur

# existing totalizer code here…

def main(scr):
   cell_width = 6
   scr.box()
   scr.refresh()

   # How many rows/cols can we fit on screen?
   rows,cols = scr.getmaxyx()
   grid_rows = (rows-4)//3
   grid_cols = cols//(cell_width+2)  # +2 for borders
```

```
    totalizer = Totalizer(scr,grid_rows,grid_cols,cell_width)
    totalizer.run()

if __name__ == "__main__": cur.wrapper(main)
```

The following screenshot (Fig 2.) of the finished application shows the help window on top of a grid with headings, some entered values and the total of a selected range displayed at the bottom. (Notice that negative numbers are handled correctly too.) The menu at the very top (File,Edit, etc) as well as the scrollbar are part of the terminal emulator GUI window not the Totalizer application.

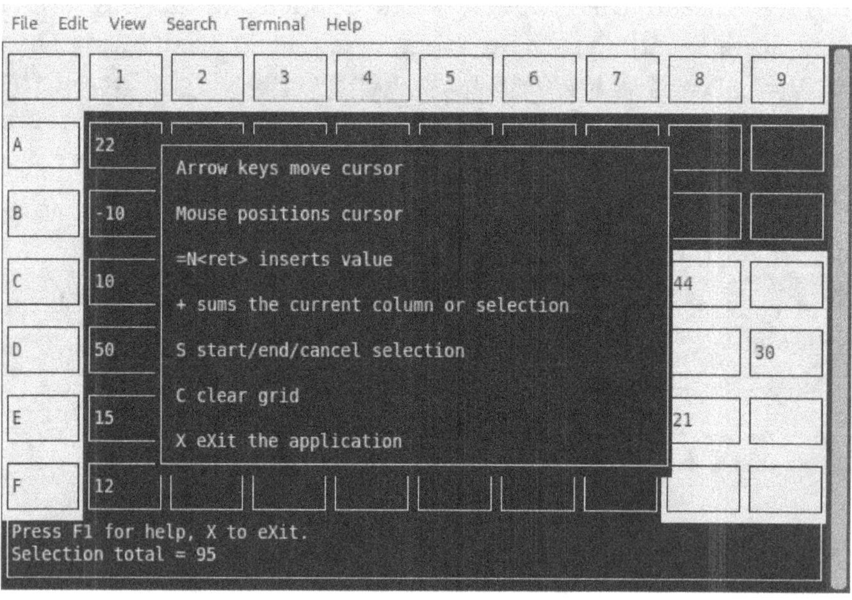

Figure 2 Totalizer Screenshot

Some Things to Consider

The code is reasonably functional, but could be improved in many ways.

- The error handling could be enhanced. For example, to prevent a Totalizer bigger than the available window being created (or any curses errors raised by the Cells could be caught).
- Extra operations could be added – for example a sort operation. File-based saving and reading could be introduced (possibly utilizing the dialog module to select folders and filenames). Ultimately, you could reinvent the spreadsheet and relive the glory days of Visicalc, Lotus 123 and Supercalc.
- A right-click mouse menu could also be introduced, especially if more operations were added. Simply pop up a new window, just as we did for the help screen, complete with the list of options, then allow the user to select one before closing the menu window again and performing the chosen operation.
- Different subclasses of `Grid` could be used to build different applications such as a text-based grid for crossword puzzles and other word games, or grids for games such as sudoku, oxo, magic square etc.
- The design of curses is not naturally conducive to the use of a Model-View-Controller (MVC) framework but with some extra effort such a framework could be constructed and thus have the data values stored completely separately from the display components. In that scenario the cells would become views of the data and the grid a view of the cells. However, creating such an architecture would involve writing almost as much code again as we have here.

All of these suggestions are left as exercises for the reader.

16. Time For Some Fun !!!

I've mentioned games as a potential curses use-case several times, so I thought it would be good to demonstrate some of those features with a classic computer game: Conway's "Game of Life", or more usually just "life".

In this game we create a starting set of living cells and then allow the cells to regenerate periodically according to a set of rules.

- A living cell continues living if it has 2 or 3 living neighbours
- An empty cell comes alive if it has exactly 3 neighbours
- All other cells die

In our implementation of the game we use `halfdelay()` mode to accept input while not blocking for too long between generation updates. We also turn off the cursor to avoid distractions.

We define a `Cell` class that holds the cell location and state information. It is purely a data receptacle with no methods of its own. We could probably do more with this class but I decided to keep things as simple as possible.

The cells are drawn on a borderless window called `scr`, which is one line shorter than `stdscr`. A second `status` window (also borderless to give the impression of a single large display area) is created on the bottom line of the screen and used to display how many generations have been produced.

The starting pattern is known as a “die-hard” and it continues to create cells for 130 generations before eventually becoming extinct. There are other standard patterns that can be used some of which live forever, or expand to fill the screen or alternate between fixed patterns. You can create your own starting patterns by modifying the `workarea` setup, just remember that if you are copying a known pattern that in curses we use Y before X!

Most of the complexity is in the `calc()` function which relies on the states being `1` and `0` to calculate the number of neighbours the cell has and then applies the rules of the game to determine each cell’s next state.

We detect the Escape key to exit. Notice that the definition for this is imported from the `curses.ascii` module because it is not one of the keys defined in the curses module. We use `halfdelay()` to prevent the program stopping and slow down the cycle rate (you can change the delay to change the generation rate).

Finally, we test the size of the terminal before commencing the game and, if it is too small, exit via a `ValueError`. The main code uses a `try/except` to catch this error and inform the user that they need to resize their terminal.

There is a function called `hasLife()` that tests to see whether there are any cells left alive and if not we terminate the event loop – since nothing new can possibly appear once all cells are dead. There are other closing states that can occur (including steady-state and cyclical states) and significantly more work will be required to detect those if desired.

```
import curses as cur
from curses.ascii import ESC

# create state constants
DEAD = 0
ALIVE = 1

class Cell:
   def __init__(self, x, y):
      self.x = x
      self.y = y
      self.oldstate = DEAD
      self.newstate = DEAD

def main(stdscr):
   scr = cur.newwin(cur.LINES-1,cur.COLS)
   cur.curs_set(0) # make cursor invisible
   Ymax,Xmax = scr.getmaxyx()

   status = cur.newwin(1,cur.COLS,cur.LINES-1,0)

   workarea = [[Cell(x,y) for x in range(Xmax)]
                for y in range(Ymax)]
   if (cur.LINES < 20 or cur.COLS < 60):
      raise ValueError

   # Set up "die-hard" pattern - lives for 130 generations.
   workarea[10][40].newstate = ALIVE
   workarea[11][34].newstate = ALIVE
   workarea[11][35].newstate = ALIVE
   workarea[12][35].newstate = ALIVE
   workarea[12][39].newstate = ALIVE
   workarea[12][40].newstate = ALIVE
   workarea[12][41].newstate = ALIVE

   update_state(workarea)
   display(scr, workarea)

   status.addstr(0,0, "Hit any key to start," +
                      " Hold Escape to exit...")
```

```
    status.getch()
    cur.halfdelay(4) # use delay to allow ESC to be read

    status.clear()
    generations = 0


    # Start the event loop
    while scr.getch() != ESC and
          hasLife(workarea):
      generations += 1
      for line in workarea:
        for cell in line:
          calc(workarea, cell)
      update_state(workarea)
      display(scr, workarea)
      status.addstr(0,0,"Generation: %d" % generations)
      status.getch()

def display(win, area):
    win.clear()
    for line in area:
      for cell in line:
        if cell.oldstate == ALIVE:
          win.addch(cell.y,cell.x, '#')
    win.refresh()

def calc(area,cell):
    x,y = cell.x,cell.y
    Ymax = len(area)
    Xmax = len(area[0])
    neighbours = area[y-1][x].oldstate
    neighbours += area[y-1][x-1].oldstate
    neighbours += area[y-1][(x+1) % Xmax].oldstate
    neighbours += area[(y+1) % Ymax][x].oldstate
    neighbours += area[(y+1) % Ymax][x-1].oldstate
    neighbours += area[(y+1) % Ymax][(x+1) % Xmax].oldstate
    neighbours += area[y][x-1].oldstate
    neighbours += area[y][(x+1) % Xmax].oldstate
```

```
    # apply the rules of the game to see what
    # the cell will look like
    if (cell.oldstate == ALIVE) and (neighbours in (2, 3)):
       next_state = ALIVE
    elif (cell.oldstate == DEAD) and (neighbours == 3):
       next_state = ALIVE
    else: next_state = DEAD
    cell.newstate = next_state


def update_state(area):
   for line in area:
     for cell in line:
       cell.oldstate = cell.newstate

# Check if cells are all dead.
def hasLife(area):
   for line in area:
      for cell in line:
        if cell.newstate == ALIVE:
           return True

try: cur.wrapper(main)
except ValueError:
       print ("Screen is too small(min: 20x60)," +
             " please resize and try again.")
```

The code for this was translated from a publicly available online C program and then adapted to Python idioms. There are many curses programs available online and we will discuss some of the practicalities of translating them to Python in the next chapter.

17. Converting from C to Python

There are many C-based curses programs available on the internet. It is not unusual to want to translate these, either whole or in part, to Python. This chapter considers some tips for performing the translation. It assumes a basic knowledge of the C language but we will not be compiling or running any of the C code included. You certainly do not need a C compiler, just a regular text editor.

While it is relatively easy to do a straight conversion of the C idioms into Python, that is not generally the best approach. Usually there will be opportunities to "tidy up" the code by adopting Python idioms. Both approaches will be discussed.

The basic structure of the chapter will follow the structure of this book. We start with initialization followed by output, input, attributes, windows and colours.

For the C examples I will use snippets from the Game of Life program mentioned in the previous chapter.

A couple of bits of general advice first though:

- Always make a copy of the C file and work on that. Then you can always go back to the original code. Ideally, if your editor supports vertical split windows load the original into a read-only buffer on one side and work on the copy in the other buffer, so the original and new code is side by side. Then if you accidentally delete too much you can see (and cut-n-paste) the original code.
- Remember to remove C type information. It is easy to accidentally leave the types in the parameter list and then get error messages from Python. Don't forget to replace the return type with the Python keyword `def`.

- Don't be afraid to adopt Python-style idioms where appropriate. For example use a Python-style `for` loop rather than `range()` and indexing.
  And use list comprehensions to initialize lists (aka arrays) if possible.

Initialization

The first thing to do is convert the C

```
#include <curses.h>
```

to

```
import curses
```

C does not have the `Python curses.wrapper()` feature, nor does it have a `try/except/finally` structure. As a consequence you will need to decide how much of the existing initialization code needs to be included in your Python program. The individual functions are all identical to their Python equivalents, but you will need to precede them with their module prefix.

One feature that C has, which is absent in Python, is the predefined `stdscr` variable. You may find it helpful to call the window returned from `initscr() stdscr`, just for convenience in translating the code. This would include the parameter name for `main()` if you decide to utilize the Python `wrapper()` function.

You may find constant definitions (either as variables or using `#define`) which are usually just replicated into Python using the convention of all uppercase variable names.

Program data may be represented in structs using `typedef`. These are usually best converted to Python classes without methods. Here is an example from the Life example:

```
typedef struct _state {
  int oldstate;
  int newstate;
} state;
```

I converted this initially to:

```
class State:
   def __init__(self):
      self.oldstate = DEAD
      self.newstate = DEAD
```

But then later, as the translation progressed I realized I could simplify the code by adding some more attributes to the class, this is fairly common in my experience.

You may also find forward declarations of functions; these can simply be deleted as not required in Python.

Finally, remember to delete the semicolons at the end of lines plus any stray braces. Stray semicolons don't generally cause any problems in Python but the braces surely will!

Output

In Python all of the output features are implemented as methods of the window class. C takes a different approach and takes a window argument as a part of the function signature. There are families of functions with varying numbers of arguments. A naming convention is used in these groups. We will look at the `addstr()` family:

```
int addstr(const char *str);
int waddstr(WINDOW *win, const char *str);
int mvaddstr(int y, int x, const char *str);
int mvwaddstr(WINDOW *win, int y, int x, const char *str);
```

All of these can be replaced by the single `addstr()` method in Python. The functions are used as follows:

- `addstr()` uses `stdscr` as its window and displays text at the current cursor position.
- `waddstr()` takes a window argument and writes to that window at the current cursor position.
- `mvaddstr()` takes a pair of coordinates and writes to `stdscr` at that location.
- `mvwaddstr()` takes a window and coordinate pair and writes to the specified window at the specified location.

The same groups of function prefixes exist for `addchr()`, `addnstr()` etc.

One group of functions that you may well encounter has no Python counterpart. That is the `printw()` group. These use C `printf()` style character formatting to create the output string. In Python we simply use string formatting and use the regular `addstr()` method to display the result. Thus a line like

```
wprintw(my_win, "The score is %d", score);
```

would translate to:

```
my_win.addstr("The score is %d" % score)
```

Input

Input functions come in the same groupings as the output functions.

For most significant curses programs the bulk of user input will be the `getch()` function. That's an easy translation to Python's `getch()` method, just remember to check that you are using the correct window object!

Attributes

There is very little difference in the use of attributes between C and Python. Even the bitwise OR operators are the same(`|`). The functions are of course grouped as before but the Python equivalent usage should be obvious.

Windows

These functions are similar to their Python equivalents. Remember that you do not need to explicitly delete windows in Python since the garbage collector, or the `del()` function, will tidy up for you. As a result you can remove (or replace with `del()`) any calls `to delwin()` that appear in the C code.

For derived and sub-windows the creation is done by methods of the parent window whereas in C the window is the first argument, as it is for all the other window management functions.

Colours

Because all the C colour handling functions are also functions in Python, it's fairly straightforward to convert the code. Just remember to add the curses module prefix for both the functions and defined constants. One oddity is the `COLOR_PAIR()` and `PAIR_NUMBER()` functions which in Python are spelled in lower case.

One small wrinkle you might encounter is that the latest versions of ncurses include extended colour handling to increase the number of colours that can be accommodated. These are not supported in Python, so you will need to do some work to downgrade any use of extended colours from C to Python.

That's really all I have to say, it's a fairly mechanistic process converting a C curses program to Python and if you have worked your way through this book you should be well equipped to work around any unusual code you come across. Remember to take advantage of Python's higher-level programming constructs to simplify the code whenever possible. Clearer code is easier to maintain and extend.

18. References

Online

- NCURSES FAQ pages http://invisible-island.net/ncurses/ncurses.faq.html
- Pradeep's original ncurses How-To document: https://www.tldp.org/HOWTO/NCURSES-Programming-HOWTO/
- Python curses module documentation: https://docs.python.org/3/library/curses.html#module-curses
- Python Panel documentation: https://docs.python.org/3/library/curses.panel.html

Also, don't forget the man pages on your OS. The curses functions are all covered under section (3) – subroutines. The pages treat related groups of functions together (eg `addstr`, `addch` etc). They only cover the native C ncurses functions, not the Python module, but the behaviours described should translate to Python. For information about the mouse try `$ man mouse` and for an overview `$ man curses`

Books

There are also a few dead-tree books on the ncurses C library that might prove useful. (I don't know of any published Python curses books.) I can personally recommend the following:

- *Dan Gookins Guide to Ncurses Programming* by Dan Gookin. Self-published on Kindle. A low-cost tutorial that covers programming ncurses in C. It only covers the core ncurses features but does so quite thoroughly.

- *Programming with Curses* by John Strang. Published by O'Reilly. Now discontinued but you may be able to pick up a used copy. It focuses on the original BSD curses library rather than ncurses so there is no discussion of text attributes, colour or mouse interaction, but for the basics of text manipulation it is pretty comprehensive. If you want to understand how curses works under the covers, this is your best bet short of reading the C source code.

Source Code

The source code for the examples in the book is available as a zip file from my web site:

http://www.alan-g.me.uk/hills/PythonCursesCode.zip

The file names should be self explanatory, matching the example numbers in the book. Any errors reported will be fixed and the zip file updated so if you run into problems it might be worth fetching the latest zip file and checking the code to see if there has been an update. The code is released under a Creative Commons license, so you are free to edit and share it as you see fit.

About the Author

Alan Gauld is a semi-retired software engineer and systems architect with over 40 years experience in the IT industry mainly working in the telecommunications sector. He has used over 20 programming languages during his career. For personal use he uses Python, which he discovered in 1998 and has used ever since. He is the moderator of the Python tutor mailing list and author of two programming books about Python.

When not programming he can often be found hiking in his native Scottish Highlands or out with his camera taking landscape photographs. He has also published a series of e-books about exploring Scotland's waterways: the canals and river walks and these are also available as a single volume traditional format book.

www.ingramcontent.com/pod-product-compliance
Lightning Source LLC
Chambersburg PA
CBHW070549220526
45467CB00003B/1138

9798708884435